Why We Do the Things We Do

Psychology in a  Nutshell

By the same author:

Freudian Slips

Why? Answers to Everyday Scientific Questions

The Infinite Tortoise

Why We Do the Things We Do

Psychology in a Nutshell

JOEL LEVY

Michael O'Mara Books Limited

To Mike and Christina,
who helped make this book possible.

This paperback edition first published in 2017

First published in Great Britain in 2015 by
Michael O'Mara Books Limited
9 Lion Yard
Tremadoc Road
London SW4 7NQ

A CIP catalogue record for this book is available from the British
Library.

Papers used by Michael O'Mara Books Limited are natural, recyclable
products made from wood grown in sustainable forests. The
manufacturing processes conform to the environmental regulations of
the country of origin.

ISBN: 978-1-78243-785-7 in paperback print format
ISBN: 978-1-78243-410-8 in ebook format

5 7 9 10 8 6 4

Designed and typeset by K.DESIGN, Winscombe, Somerset

Printed and bound by CPI Group (UK) Ltd, Croydon CR0 4YY

www.mombooks.com

Contents

Introduction: where did psychology come from?

Psychology is the study of the mind. The word itself comes from the Greek root *psyche*, meaning 'the mind or soul', and the suffix –ology, from the Greek *logos*, meaning 'the study of'. The term 'psychology' was not coined until around the sixteenth century and only came into popular use in the eighteenth century. In fact, psychology was not practised as an explicitly identified discipline until the late nineteenth century. Its roots, however, can be traced back much further than this.

Folk psychology

All humans are what might be termed folk or naïve psychologists, in that everyone considers, interprets and predicts their own and other people's thoughts and behaviour. The ability to surmise what might be going through other people's minds and modify your own thinking and behaviour accordingly is sometimes called social intelligence. There is a school of thought that human intelligence in general arose from the evolution of social intelligence. The term 'theory of mind' has a specific meaning in relation to interpersonal psychology, describing the ability to think about what other people are thinking. This is seen as an essential tool for normal interpersonal relations, and an inability to formulate a theory of mind is linked to autistic spectrum disorders (*see* page 135). So our everyday 'psychologizing' could be said to lie at the root of what makes us – and has made us – human.

Body and brain

As a practice in the academic or professional sense, precursors of psychology can be identified in pre-modern and alternative models of the psyche and its relation to the world. In Ancient Greece, for instance, a form of dream therapy was practised 2,500 years before Jung (*see* page 50), in healing temples where sick people would pray and make offerings before 'incubating' dreams that delivered divine guidance and intercession as they slept (*see* page 16 for more on this).

Ancient Greek medicine reflected aspects of what today is known as a holistic approach, recognizing

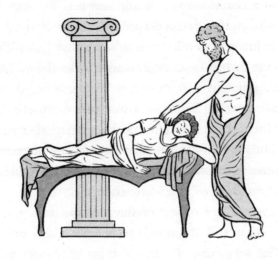

the role of the psyche in determining bodily health. Medieval and Early Modern medicine developed from Classical antecedents and reflected this psychological element in theories such as the four 'humours' – blood, phlegm, black bile and yellow bile – that were said to govern mood and character. Mental illness was likewise primarily viewed as an expression of physiological imbalances.

Contrary to popular belief, demonic possession was *not* the most common cause to which insanity was attributed. Evidence from records of medieval 'inquisitions' (that is, inquests to determine sanity, aka 'idiocy') show that there was generally a clear view of madness as having physical, bodily causes, with almost no appeal to supernatural agency. 'Madness was overwhelmingly perceived as a disorder of the body and brain,' points out medieval historian David Roffe ('Perceptions of insanity in medieval England', 1998). Where possible, specific causes were attributed – for example, in 1309 Bartholemew de Sakeville was said to have become an idiot after developing an acute fever, while in 1349 Robert de Irthlingborough was found to have lost his memory and gone insane after he had been struck on the head by a lance while jousting.

Although this model of the physiological basis of psychology still informed psychiatric thinking and practice into the eighteenth century, humoral theory had begun to fall out of favour from the Renaissance onward. Increased enthusiasm for anatomical dissection, starting with Andreas Vesalius in the sixteenth century, found illness increasingly localized in specific sites of the body, so that 'lesions' or disruptions of specific tissues replaced humoral imbalance as the cause of disease. At the same time there was an increasing emphasis on emotional states as a cause of mental illness in themselves: for example, grief as a cause of melancholy, or terror as a cause of hysteria. Yet even today, terms such as phlegmatic or sanguine are still used to characterize temperament and personality, demonstrating the long reach of the theory of the four humours.

Thus psychology was linked to physiology. In the

sixteenth and seventeenth centuries, works such as Montaigne's *Essays* (1580), Robert Burton's *The Anatomy of Melancholy* (1621) and Shakespeare's plays (1590–1613) saw an increasing emphasis on the inner life of the mind, but there was little separation between psychology and philosophy.

A scientific approach

Our modern conception of psychology arose from movements such as mesmerism and phrenology (*see* pages 20 and 23). Though now recognized as pseudosciences, these approaches did much to advance and legitimize medical and scientific study of the mind. The genesis of psychological science can be traced back to the laboratories of Wilhelm Wundt, who in 1879 opened the Institute for Experimental Psychology at the University of Leipzig in Germany. Wundt's background was in medicine, and he was determined to put psychology on a scientific footing, having learned what is now called psychophysics from his teacher Hermann von Helmholtz. Psychophysics is the study of the response of the nervous system to physical stimuli. Helmholtz investigated topics such as the levels at which luminosity of light or loudness of sound become perceptible, and the speed of transmission of electrical impulses in nerves.

Wundt tried to apply similar techniques of quantification and precise measurement to the inner realms of the mind through a technique known as introspection, which involved the experimenter reporting on his own perceptions and thoughts. Wundt's aim was to analyse perception, sensation and thought into their component parts or structures, giving rise to the school of psychology known as structuralism. Wundt tried to get around the inevitable subjectivity of introspection by training his students to be as precise as possible, but the inherent flaws in this technique eventually led to its devastating critique at the hands of the succeeding behaviourist school of psychology (*see* page 30).

James and functionalism

Around the same time as Wundt was working in Germany, the physician, philosopher and psychologist William James was also developing psychology in the United States. His approach stressed the functions (which is to say, purpose and utility) of behaviour and thoughts, and so his school came to be known as functionalism. Perhaps James's greatest contribution to psychology was his landmark 1890 textbook *The Principles of Psychology*, which set out themes of psychology that are still current today, such as brain function, consciousness and the self, perception, instinct, memory and emotion. Later, James somewhat disavowed psychology and his famous book, preferring philosophy, but the definition that he set out in the *Principles* remains one of the best known:

Psychology is the Science of Mental Life, both of its phenomena and of their conditions . . . The Phenomena are such things as we call feelings, desires, cognition, reasoning, decisions and the like.

Joel Levy

What happened to mad people in Ancient Greece?

The psychology of prehistoric peoples is hard to study because it can only be inferred from archeological remains. In terms of psychiatry (the medical treatment of people with mental illness or disorders), the most striking evidence from prehistory comes from skulls that had been drilled with holes. This is known as trepanation or trephination, and the traditional interpretation is that it indicated widespread belief that mental illness was due to bad spirits, which could be released or exorcized by providing a physical outlet; hence the hole. It is equally if not more plausible, however, that trepanation was performed for straightforward and clinically appropriate reasons, such as relieving pressure caused by blows to the head, or removing splinters or blood clots from the same cause.

It is ⌐
of other
was comm⌐
in the Bronze
from the Book ⌐
Lord troubled [Sa⌐
him, Behold now, an
thee.' In the Bible, music ⌐   a
'cunning player on the harp   wever,
exorcism was brutal and trau⌐   ⌐ng sonic
and physical torture, beatings, s⌐   ⌐n and other
torments intended to drive out de⌐⌐ons. Tragically,
such abhorrent methods are still applied today by
fundamentalist believers in demonic possession.

Ancient Greek myths and legends report similarly magical treatments for mental illness. The legendary healer Melampus cured Iphicles of impotence by a kind of proto-Freudian analysis, in which the roots of his disorder are traced back to an incident in which Iphicles was scared by his father wielding a bloody knife that he had used in animal sacrifice. In the Greek legend the knife was inadvertently stabbed into a tree nymph, who then cursed Iphicles. Melampus cured Iphicles by freeing the blade and making him drink a potion of water and the rust from its blade.

healer was Asclepius, who became
edicine. At temples dedicated to his cult,
ck were treated with a form of dream therapy,
again anticipating psychoanalytic techniques from
over 2,000 years later. Troubled patients would relax
in the soothing environment of the temple and then
'incubate' dreams by praying to the gods before going
to sleep in a dormitory known as an *enkoimeteria* or a
subterranean chamber called the *abaton*. The resulting
dreams were interpreted – with the help of priestly
therapists – to suggest treatments. Asclepion dream
temples specialized in different ailments: the sanctuary
at Tricca treated hysteria, that at Epidaurus cured
mental disorders with the blood of Medusa, and in
Megara they healed emotional disturbances.

All in the head

Eventually the attribution of mental illness to
supernatural agency was supplemented with a model
that emphasized natural causes, particularly in the
school of Hippocrates (460–377 BCE). He attributed
mental disorders to physiological problems rather
than magical or mystical elements, and located those
problems in the brain. Mental illness was linked to

imbalances in the four humours (types of fluid) that governed personality and mood (*see* page 10), and these were linked to the classification system for mental disorders that Classical medicine developed, aspects of which are still current.

The Ancient Greeks and Romans characterized a number of mental conditions. These include mania, a state of euphoria and frenzy; melancholia, which is similar to what is today called depression; hysteria, manifested in physical symptoms without obvious physical causes (today known as conversion disorder); and dementia, or general intellectual decline. They also distinguished between hallucinations (seeing, hearing and otherwise sensing things that aren't there) and delusions (false beliefs).

Humane and rational treatments for psychological problems were also proposed. Hippocrates recommended measures such as quiet living, healthy diet and exercise, and later Greek and Roman physicians employed music, massage, baths and a soothing, supportive environment. The second-century Graeco-Roman physician Galen even distinguished between medical causes, such as head injuries and alcohol, and emotional causes, such as grief or stress, for mental illness. The statesman and writer Cicero developed a questionnaire for the assessment of mental illness that resembles modern diagnostic tools, including questions on *habitus* (appearance), *orationes* (speech), and *casus* (significant life events).

Can you really tell a criminal by the bumps on his head?

The answer to this question is 'probably not', but this was one of the claims of the pseudoscience of phrenology (from the Greek for 'study of the mind'), which was popular from the late eighteenth to late nineteenth centuries. Phrenology was predicated on a series of core beliefs:

- 'The brain is the organ of the mind': in other words, the mind arises from, and is located solely within, the brain.
- Distinct mental faculties, such as 'destructiveness' and 'benevolence', are localized in specific parts or 'organs' of the brain.
- The larger the brain organ, the more powerful and more dominant the faculty.
- The 'doctrine of the skull': there is a direct correlation between the shape of the brain and the

shape of the skull, or in the words of the leading phrenologist Johann Kaspar Spurzheim (1776–1832), 'the form of the internal surface of the skull is determined by the external form of the brain . . . while the external surface of the skull agrees with its internal surface'.

Thus, specific organs correlate directly to specific skull 'protuberances', or bumps. Measuring or gauging these bumps makes it possible to determine the strength of the faculties in an individual. In other words, the bumps on a person's head can be read to reveal their character, traits and abilities.

Organology

Phrenology originated with the work of eighteenth-century Viennese physician and anatomist Franz Joseph Gall, although he did not use the term, which was coined in 1815 by the British physician T. I. M. Forster. Personal experience had suggested to Gall a link between bulging eyes and good memory, and he started to look for other links between physical features and mental faculties, eventually settling on the skull and brain. Gall's brilliant anatomical work lent credence to what he called 'organology', or simply 'the physiology of the brain', but it was his student

Spurzheim who became the great apostle for the new discipline. Spurzheim was a compelling lecturer and stressed the positive ramifications of what he and Gall considered to be a new science, including the possibility of training the faculties and thus effecting self-improvement.

The science of man

The promise of self-improvement helped to turn phrenology into a popular movement, even as it lost credibility in scientific circles. In Scotland, Spurzheim's gospel was avidly taken up by the moral philosopher George Combe, who went on to popularize phrenology in Britain and the United States. Phrenology chimed with the emerging and increasingly self-educated middle and artisan classes and their appetite for a rational but accessible new 'science of man', as Combe termed it. Many journals boosted the new science, including Combe's own *Phrenological Journal* from 1823, and by 1832 there were twenty-nine phrenological societies in Britain alone. In 1846, Combe was invited to London to read the bumps of Queen Victoria's children at Buckingham Palace.

Gall had posited twenty-seven faculties, ranging from the 'impulse to propagation' and 'tenderness to progeny' to 'larceny' and 'religious sentiment'. Spurzheim inflated these to thirty-three; Combe increased this to thirty-five; and later phrenologists suggested up to forty-three faculties. A system of classification was developed, with a hierarchy from 'propensities', shared with the animals, to higher intellectual faculties. While Gall favoured using the palms to 'read' bumps on the head, more common practice was to use the fingers. Phrenologists eventually offered customers a checklist of faculties, individually rated on a scale of 2 to 7, and marked as requiring either 'cultivation' or 'restraint', together with a book of exercises for achieving just these outcomes.

The midwife of psychology

Today phrenology has become a byword for pseudoscience, and even in its own day the practice was widely lampooned. Traditionally, historians of psychology dismissed it as an aberration, 'an embarrassing *faux pas*', in the words of J. C. Flügel, former president of the British Psychological Society (1932–5). Increasingly, however, phrenology is coming to be seen as a sort of proto-psychology, prefiguring many of the themes that are current in modern psychology.

Phrenologists were the first to suggest localization of brain function – the idea that specific mental abilities relate to specific parts of the brain, an idea now central to neuropsychology, although the extreme specificity of phrenology has been rejected. The notion that the outside of the skull relates to the shape of the brain inside it, and that this in turn has anything to do with specific mental faculties, is now widely ridiculed. However, paleoanthropologists (who study prehistoric humans) have used measurements of bumps on the inside of prehistoric skulls to show the enlargement of brain structures said to be 'language areas', and thus draw conclusions about the evolution of human language abilities. The phrenologist's concept of faculties has also had many parallels in psychology, from Chomsky's 'language acquisition' module (*see* page 82), to the traits of personality psychology (*see* page 96). More generally, phrenology, along with mesmerism (*see* page 23), is now credited with advancing new ideas and approaches to the study of the mind, based at least in part on evidence and scientific principles, and so acting as a sort of midwife to the science of psychology.

Is hypnosis for real?

Despite over 200 years of study, there is still no definitive understanding of what hypnosis is or how it might work. In fact, opinion remains divided over whether there is any such thing as hypnosis, at least in the popular sense. But hypnosis played an important role in the emergence of psychology.

Animal magnetism

Shortly before the advent of phrenology, Europe was swept by another enthusiasm later dismissed as a pseudoscience practised by charlatans: mesmerism, named after the Austrian physician Franz Anton Mesmer (1734–1815). Mesmer won his doctorate in 1766 with a thesis that attempted to apply to human physiology the newly popular theories of Isaac Newton and his invisible but cosmic force, gravity, suggesting that there was such a thing as 'animal gravity'. Encountering the use of iron magnets as medical cures, Mesmer developed his animal gravity into 'animal magnetism', a mysterious, fluidic force akin to normal magnetism, but which flowed through and between living things. Manipulation of this fluid force, through the use of Mesmer's own hands or magnetized iron rods, could cure a range of problems, both physical and psychological.

Mesmer achieved great success and fame in Vienna, but hostility from the medical establishment prompted him to move to Paris in 1778. There, he caused a sensation and was so in demand that he had to invent a device allowing him to treat multiple patients at once. This device, which he called a *bacquet*, came in the form of a tub fitted with bottles of 'magnetized' water and iron filings, which powered human circuits of a 'magnetized circle', or a ring of people holding hands and sitting inside the tub. Mesmer's barrel and his charismatic presence produced extraordinary effects on his clients, particularly the ladies. His popularity also inspired an increasing host of imitators.

In 1784 a Royal Academy of Sciences inquiry, headed by American Founding Father and scientist Benjamin Franklin, concluded that animal magnetism did not exist and that mesmerism acted by suggestibility alone. Mesmer left Paris and eventually faded into obscurity, but mesmerism nonetheless spread across Europe and to the Americas.

Magnetic sleep

One particularly important development was the discovery, by the most important of Mesmer's followers, the Marquis de Puységur (1751–1825), of what he called 'magnetic sleep', which became known as somnambulism, and which would now be called a hypnotic trance. This is an apparently distinct state of consciousness in which a person acts like a sleepwalker. Puységur attributed psychic powers to the somnambulist, and noted his amnesia for the experience. Magnetic sleep became the primary focus of mesmerism, shifting its focus from the body to the mind.

This new psychological direction was adopted by Scottish physician James Braid (1795–1860), who coined the term hypnosis from the Greek word for sleep, *hypnos*, after emphasizing the similarities between mesmeric states and sleep. Braid developed a new technique for hypnotizing someone: getting them to focus on a single idea, initially by staring at an object (hence the popular image of hypnotic trance induced by a swinging pendulum).

In France, Braid's ideas were taken up at the influential Salpêtrière Institute in Paris, where the pioneering psychiatrist Jean-Martin Charcot (1825–93) came to believe that hypnosis is related to the amnesia and paralysis displayed in some forms of psychosis.

Hypnosis became an important tool in the treatment of psychiatric disorders and helped to lead Sigmund Freud to develop the concept of the unconscious, but a dispute arose over the nature of this strange phenomenon. Charcot's followers, primarily Pierre Janet, developed the concept of hypnosis as a special state involving some degree of dissociation of consciousness (with some parts of the mind or personality 'going to sleep' while others continued to function). By contrast, Hippolyte Bernheim (1840–1919), a professor of medicine in Nancy, France, argued that hypnosis is based on normal psychological processes to do with suggestion and suggestibility.

State or non-state?

These contrasting positions over the nature of hypnosis persist today. The dominant academic view, descending from Bernheim, is the 'non-state' hypothesis, which holds that hypnosis is not a distinct state. Instead it is seen as a kind of learned behaviour, a sort of act performed according to an unconscious script. Yet the popular concept of hypnosis persists, in which it is viewed in much the same terms as the Marquis de Puységur's somnambulism: a quasi-mystical, altered state of consciousness in which strange phenomena become possible.

Is free will an illusion?

When you make a decision or perform an action it certainly feels like you choose to do so, and could have made another choice if you wanted. For instance, if confronted with a piece of rotten meat, you would probably choose not to eat it, but you could have chosen to eat it, making such a choice of your own free will. Or could you?

There is a strong school of thought called determinism, which suggests that your action is determined by pre-existing factors, such as having learned through bitter experience that rotten meat makes you sick, or natural instincts evolved over millions of years that are stimulated by the sight and smell of decay and trigger a disgust response. Thus, your behaviour could have been predicted, and any belief that you could have chosen otherwise is simply an illusion.

The ghost in the machine

The debate between free will and determinism is one of the most profound questions in philosophy, but it is not simply a matter for scholars in ivory towers. It goes to the core of whether psychology is or can be a science, which itself was the defining question of the birth of psychology. The whole point of psychology is to explore a scientific way of looking at mind and behaviour, and it started when the study of the mind moved beyond philosophy and into the laboratory of Wilhelm Wundt (*see* page 11), in 1879.

A fundamental contradiction lay at the heart of Wundt's project, however. He wanted to claim the trappings and rigour of science for psychology, but his subject matter was the internal workings of the mind, which he tried to interrogate through the method of introspection. Wundt believed that discipline and training could give the introspector sufficient rigour to achieve an objective account of his internal life, but this was a fallacy: introspection could only be subjective.

In fact, the concept of free will poses a deeper problem for psychology's claim to be a science. A scientific account of a phenomenon requires some degree of consistency and predictability. Any ball dropped from any tower will accelerate at the same rate; water at standard temperature and pressure will always boil at 100°C (212°F) and freeze at 0°C (32°F). If the variables are the same, the experiment can be replicated and the outcome will be the same. But free will means that identical variables can lead to completely opposite outcomes. Philosopher Ted Honderich defines the doctrine of free will as saying that 'on a given occasion, with the past just as it was and the present and ourselves just as they are, we can choose or decide the opposite of what we actually do choose or decide' (*How Free Are You*, 2002). Because the mechanism of free will is unknowable, it is not open to any kind of scientific investigation. Free will is like the ghost in the machine of the mind, affecting its workings in mysterious ways.

Pavlov's dogs

Considerations such as the free will versus determinism debate led to a wholesale rejection of Wundt's introspection by the movement called behaviourism, whose members restricted their study to observable psychological phenomena – behaviour – rather than the impossible-to-observe internal phenomena of thinking. Behaviourism was inspired by the famous experiments of Ivan Pavlov, which showed that dogs could be conditioned to reliably and predictably produce the same type of response (salivating) in response to the same stimulus (a bell ringing). Pavlov's experiments could be expressed in formulae similar to those of chemistry or mathematics; for example, neutral stimulus associated with unconditioned stimulus provokes unconditioned response, becomes NS + UCS = UCR.

Pavlov's demonstration of conditioning, a learning process by which an organism (whether human or animal) is trained to produce a specific behaviour in response to a specific stimulus, prompted American psychologist John B. Watson to declare a new approach to psychology with his 1913 manifesto, 'Psychology as the Behaviourist Views It'. In this article, Watson insists that psychology should be 'a purely objective natural science' and rejects 'interpretation in terms of consciousness'. Behaviourism became the dominant paradigm for psychology up until the 1960s, and remains important today.

Are criminals responsible for their actions?

Watson's student B. F. Skinner later became the arch-proponent of behaviourism, developing what he called 'radical behaviourism'. He rejected the concept of free will as an illusion in his book, *Beyond Freedom and Dignity* (1971), claimimg that traditional views of the autonomy of the person had to be re-examined in the light of 'controlling relations between behaviour and environment' revealed by science. In other words, all our normal conceptions of responsibility, including criminal responsibility, should be re-examined. Skinner applied his reasoning to his own life, insisting, 'I did not direct my life. I didn't design it. I never made decisions. Things always came up and made them for me. That's what life is.'

Soft determinism

Skinner's stark rejection of human autonomy, which relegates consciousness to the status of a side effect or illusion, was rejected by many other movements in psychology and fell out of favour. But the challenge posed by free will to psychology's claims to be a science remains. Today most psychologists adopt a position known as 'soft determinism', where it is accepted that individuals actively respond to internal and external influences, but that their choices are always informed by some degree of biological or environmental pressure.

When is a cigar not a cigar?

Sigmund Freud is popularly supposed to have said that 'sometimes a cigar is just a cigar'. In fact there is no record of him ever having said that, and the phrase itself first appeared in print in the 1950s, long after his death. What Freud did say, however, was that objects such as cigars – and practically anything else you can think of – act as symbolic representations of the phallus, or penis, for the unconscious mind. So the short answer to this question is that a cigar is not a cigar when it's a phallic symbol.

Freud's theory of the unconscious, phallic symbols and all, represented a major development in the history of psychology, with profound influence on wider human culture and society. Paradoxically, the impact of psychoanalysis, Freud's philosophy of psychology and method of treatment, today is greater outside psychology than within it.

The cathartic method

Freud came from the tradition of Helmholtz and psychophysics (*see* page 11), with a background in neurology and medicine. An Austrian Jew, his ambition to be a research scientist was thwarted by anti-Semitism, and in 1885 he moved to Paris to study under Charcot and learn hypnosis. Freud wanted to understand what caused, and how to treat, neurological disorders in which patients displayed physical symptoms without any underlying physical disease (known as 'functional disorders'). Hypnosis helped Freud begin to uncover the psychology behind such symptoms, but he found that not everyone is susceptible to its methods.

Instead, Freud turned to an approach used by another Viennese doctor and neurophysiologist, his mentor Josef Breuer. Breuer used a talking cure he called the 'cathartic method', which Freud developed into 'free association'. This is where the patient speaks aloud ideas as soon as they occur, following on from one another with as little conscious self-editing as possible. Freud believed that the associations revealed feelings, desires, anxieties and drives not accessible to the conscious mind.

Psychoanalysis and the unconscious

Through observations of himself and his patients, Freud began to formulate an all-encompassing theory of personality and psychic development that could be used to inform psychotherapy, but also explain every aspect of human culture. He set out his evolving theory in a series of landmark works at the start of the twentieth century, including *The Interpretation of Dreams* (1899), *The Psychopathology of Everyday Life* (1901) and *Three Essays on the Theory of Sexuality* (1905).

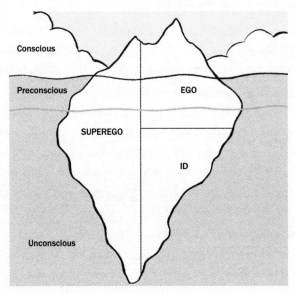

Freud viewed the human personality as being like an iceberg, the vast bulk of which lies beneath the surface of consciousness. As such, it is not accessible to conscious interrogation, but governs the conscious mind nonetheless. In this dark realm lurk all manner of thoughts and feelings too dangerous or transgressive for the conscious mind to admit to the light, yet they often swim to the surface. When this happens they appear in the conscious mind as symbols, and this is especially likely to happen in dreams, free associations, daydreams and fantasies.

Phallic symbols

Since the penis is one of the central elements of Freud's system, he and his followers tended to interpret an extraordinary range of symbols as phallic. Freud himself believed that anything from an umbrella to a hanging lamp to a Zeppelin could be a phallic symbol, while cigars themselves were indeed interpreted as phallic symbols. Eric Hiller reported in the *International Journal of Psycho-Analysis* in 1922 that: 'Cigarettes and cigars can symbolize the penis . . . They emit smoke . . . = semen . . . [The cigar] is thus a substitute for the penis . . .' Freud once admitted that his cigar smoking (which would eventually result in oral cancer) might be some sort of compensation for the compulsive masturbation of his childhood.

Freud's complex and controversial model of personality and its development divided personality into the 'id', a raging storm of infantile and animal drives and desires; the 'superego', roughly equivalent to the conscience; and the 'ego', the executive module, which tries to balance the demands of the id, the superego and the external world. Freud claimed that the infant mind is all id, with the ego developing through conflict with the external world, and the superego resulting from the psychic trauma associated with learning about male and female genitalia.

Though now dismissed within psychology as a pseudoscientific account with little basis in evidence, Freud's system engendered a powerful therapeutic tool in the shape of psychoanalytic psychotherapy. His theories spread to Britain and America and infiltrated every corner of culture, from literary criticism to Hollywood movies and television advertising. Many of his creations, and those of his followers such as Carl Jung and Alfred Adler, have entered popular culture, from the 'Freudian slip' to the 'inferiority complex'.

How does that make you feel?

In 1966 German-American computer scientist Joseph Weizenbaum used a simple program of just 200 lines of code to create 'ELIZA', one of the first ever 'chatbots' – an artificial simulacrum of someone you could have a conversation with by typing words into a computer. ELIZA recreates a very specific form of conversation: that between a humanistic or person-centred therapist and a client. The ELIZA program simply took fragments of the human user's responses and rephrased them as questions, achieving a dramatically simplified version of the humanistic psychotherapy tool known as 'reflective listening'. So, if you typed 'I feel sad', for instance, ELIZA might respond by saying 'How long have you been sad?'

Extreme disclosure

Although equipped with some clever tricks for getting out of trouble such as changing the subject or asking the human user to clarify, ELIZA is highly restricted and at best a crude simulacrum of a therapist. Yet the program proved incredibly successful at convincing users they were interacting with a real therapist, and at eliciting their extreme disclosure. Weizenbaum found that non-technical staff in his office, including his secretary, would spend hours revealing personal problems to the program. When he pointed out to his secretary that he could read all her conversations with the chatbot, he was shocked to discover how angry she was at the invasion of her privacy, as well as the way in which a real person could create such a profound connection to a few lines of computer code.

ELIZA has been taken as a trenchant critique of the psychotherapeutic style it was built to mimic. In fact, anyone can parody reflective listening therapy simply by asking someone, 'How does that make you feel?', and then repeating the question in response to every answer. Yet humanistic psychology was a major development in the history of psychology, and arguably remains the dominant paradigm for psychotherapy today. So what is behind it?

The Third Force

Humanistic psychology started as a reaction both to behaviourism's flat rejection of free will and consciousness, and to Freud's gloomy depiction of life as a battle between unsavoury drives and furtive complexes. Both of these schools of thought are more or less deterministic, and the humanistic psychologists sought what Abraham Maslow explicitly called a 'Third Force', which respected the individual's autonomy and sense of self. British psychologist John Cohen's book *Humanistic Psychology* (1958) gave the movement one of its names, but as a form of therapy it is also known as person- or client-centred therapy. Its best-known exponent was American psychotherapist Carl Rogers, who sought to redirect psychology towards human experience, meaning and choice.

Humanistic psychology is generally more positive than the two schools it opposed, behaviourism and psychoanalysis, emphasizing the individual's potential to achieve self-actualization (the goal of becoming a fulfilled and psychologically integrated person). Its critics say that humanistic psychology is philosophy, not science, constructed without evidence and impossible to test.

The hierarchy of needs

Abraham Maslow developed the hierarchy of needs, a model that describes the needs that motivate behaviour, generate values and give meaning to life.

Basic needs range from simple physical ones, such as food and safety, to slightly more complex ones such as self-esteem and the need to be loved. Higher or 'meta-' needs, including justice, autonomy, wholeness and beauty, contribute to the ultimate human goal of self-actualization, which requires qualities ranging from a sense of humour to profound self-reliance. Beyond even this come needs such as discovery, transcendence and aesthetics, which can lead to peak experiences: moments of transcendence and harmony, also known as an oceanic feeling.

What makes us happy?

Versions of this question have been the affair of philosophers since Classical times, yet have been startlingly absent from the concerns of psychology for most of its history. However, starting in the 1980s and gathering pace in the new millennium, the psychology of happiness – variously known as positive psychology, optimal psychology and well-being therapy – has become one of the fastest growing and most exciting and innovative pursuits in the field.

Flow and the Beautiful People

The roots of positive psychology lie in Maslow's 'Third Force' movement (*see* page 39). This identified as the ultimate aspirations of human psychology self-actualization, peak experience, and transcendence into what Maslow called the 'Z realm'. Hungarian-American psychologist (and positive psychology guru) Mihaly Csikszentmihalyi developed the concept of peak experiences into that of 'flow' in the 1980s and 1990s.

Other strands of humanistic psychology developed similar or related concepts. In 1961, Carl Rogers described the 'fully functioning person' as someone in touch with their deepest feelings, which Rogers called 'organismic experiences'. In 1968, clinical psychologist Dr Ted Landsman described the 'Beautiful and Noble Person', an archetype of the optimally functioning human. Despite these antecedents, psychology remained overwhelmingly focused on more negative aspects of human psychology, such as mental illness, anxiety, prejudice and bias. An analysis by Harvard psychiatrist George E. Vaillant of what he describes as 'a standard psychiatric textbook used by psychiatrists and clinical psychologists', identified that, out of the roughly one million lines of text, just five discussed hope and one joy, without a single mention of love or compassion.

Build what's strong

Partly in response to this negative bias, one of the key architects of positive psychology, University of Pennsylvania psychologist Martin E. P. Seligman, set out to add an approach he describes as 'build what's strong', to the 'fix what's wrong' programme that is standard in traditional psychotherapy. Seligman's positive psychotherapy seeks to help clients build positive emotion, strength of character and a sense of meaning. In his book *Flourish* (2011) he developed a model he called PERMA, an acronym for positive emotion, engagement, relationships, meaning and accomplishment – the elements of a fulfilled life. A related approach is 'well-being therapy', developed by Giovanni Fava MD at the University of Bologna in Italy, which proposes six tenets for happiness: mastery of the environment, personal growth, purpose in life, autonomy, self-acceptance and positive relationships.

Research backs up the efficacy and validity of positive psychology. Seligman's therapeutic methods held up to scrutiny in double-blind trials (the most rigorous test), and at least one major study shows that happiness is related to longevity. A 2012 study based on the English Longitudinal Study of Aging, which, since 2002 has gathered data on health and well-being in 11,000 people over fifty, showed that greater enjoyment in life was associated with a 28 per cent lower risk of death.

Get positive

Try these exercises and tips from positive psychology:

- Make a list of good stuff: instead of a 'to-do' list, write an 'I did it' list. Seligman advises clients to sit down every evening and write down at least three good things that happened and why.

- Accentuate the positive: Seligman has devised a questionnaire measuring twenty-four character strengths. Identify your own top five strengths, positive qualities or emotions and write them down.

- Practise your strengths: use at least one of your top strengths at least once a day.

- Say thanks: acknowledging the positive in others makes them feel better, and makes you feel better. Seligman advises making 'gratitude visits', in which you write a letter to someone explaining how grateful you are for something positive they did, and then read it to them (either in person or on the phone).

Why do we sleep?

The short answer is that nobody knows why we sleep, although there are many theories that are more or less supported by the evidence. All theories struggle to explain the key characteristic of sleep, which is that it is physiologically and neurologically different from simply resting. This is to say, sleep is a special and distinct state of consciousness, during which the body, brain and mind behave in unique ways.

REM sleep

The main changes that sleep brings are in the level and pattern of brain activity, and a general reduction in the levels of most – but not all – bodily processes. However, this overall picture is complicated by the fact that mammals (including humans) and birds experience two distinct phases of sleep: rapid eye movement (REM) sleep and non-REM (NREM) sleep. The former is characterized by greater arousal of the brain and many body systems, while the latter is generally much more subdued.

The existence of REM sleep poses a big problem to theories of sleep that suggest its function is to conserve energy and mental resources, since REM sleep does the opposite. In fact, it is a common misconception that sleep involves the shutting down of brain and body processes. There is no evidence that any major organ or system in the body shuts down during sleep: it is an active process.

One thing we know for certain is that sleep is as essential to survival as eating. Rats deprived of sleep will die within two to three weeks, roughly the same length of time it takes them to starve. Even deprivation of REM sleep alone is eventually fatal: rats with a normal lifespan of two to three years will survive just five months when deprived of REM sleep.

Sleep pressure

Humans who try to stay awake experience 'sleep pressure'; an increasingly powerful urge to sleep. Sleep pressure builds up during the day, becoming extremely hard to resist by the time you've been awake for sixteen hours, but once you go to sleep it quickly drops off and is reset back to zero. The actual mechanism behind this is mysterious, but one important chemical signal, the molecule adenosine, appears to be an important sleepiness agent. Caffeine binds to and blocks adenosine receptors (switch-like structures on nerve cells that can be 'turned on' by adenosine, in turn affecting the signalling of the nerve cells), which seems to be one of the ways that caffeine disrupts and slows the build-up of sleep pressure and increases alertness.

Sleep seems to be ubiquitous. Almost all animals have been found to sleep in one form or another, although it is hard to compare insect and fish sleep with that of reptiles, mammals and birds, because brain activity is so different in these animals. Yet even the humble fruit fly is affected by sleep-disrupting agents, in a similar fashion to mammals. Some animals, such as dolphins, can keep one side of their brain awake while the other sleeps; presumably so that they don't drown.

Necessary but not sufficient

Animals that are prevented from sleeping become ill, with suppressed immune systems and wounds that won't heal. People who get sick need to sleep more. Evidence such as this suggests that sleep is important for the body to recuperate, and that it allows the body to husband resources. Animals that use higher rates of energy sleep more. People who are prevented from sleeping, especially those kept from REM sleep, experience memory problems and poor thinking, which indicates that sleep helps with the processing of memories and with learning. Infants sleep more than adults, which implies that sleep is important for brain development. In other words, there is evidence that sleep is necessary for many functions, yet there is no single theory that is sufficient to explain all aspects of sleep.

Why do we dream?

As with sleep, dreaming is a profoundly important psychological phenomenon that resists explanation. Nobody knows why we dream, the claims of Freud notwithstanding. But, from the 1950s, laboratory investigations of dreaming have revealed the fascinating physical aspects of dreaming.

The royal road

Ancient physicians used dreams as a psychological tool in their therapy, encouraging or 'incubating' dreams at dream temples (*see* page 16). Dreaming became central in psychology with the work of Sigmund Freud, who held that 'The interpretation of dreams is the royal road to a knowledge of the unconscious activities of the mind.' Carl Jung believed that in dreams the individual psyche had access to the collective unconscious, so that archetypes could roam the dreamscape, disguised in various shapes and forms. The psychoanalytic theory of dreams regarded them as the necessary manifestations of the unconscious; a sort of sandbox in which urges and fantasies, fears and wishes, could play out and, crucially, during which anxieties and conflicts could be worked through and resolved.

The neuroscience of dreaming

Yet Freud and the psychoanalysts knew little about the actual mechanics of dreaming, and it wasn't until a series of breakthrough studies in the late 1950s that the neuroscience of dreaming began to be discovered. The so-called 'Father of American sleep research', Dr Nathaniel Kleitman, discovered REM sleep (*see* page 46) in 1953, and in 1957 he and William Dement proved that REM sleep is closely associated with dreaming (*see* page 53).

Since then, research has uncovered many important features of dreaming. For instance, we now know that dreams typically feature issues currently concerning the dreamer, including aspects of daily life such as news events, musical practice and domestic stress. Dreams are typically first person and tend to be highly emotional, particularly featuring negative emotions. Despite this highly emotional content, about 99 per cent of dreams are forgotten within moments of waking.

This last finding casts into question the psycho-analytic explanation of dreaming. If dreams function to help us resolve conflicts and overcome anxieties, would it not help to remember them? A more modern spin on the psychoanalytic view of the dream state as a psychic sandbox is to see them as a kind of virtual-reality simulator, offering the mind, particularly its less conscious aspects, the chance to run through threat scenarios as a kind of training device.

When do we dream?

In 1957, at a sleep laboratory at Stanford University, William Dement and Nathaniel Kleitman set out to discover whether they were correct in their hypothesis that dreaming happens during REM sleep. They recruited seven men and two women, hooked them up to scalp electrodes to measure their brain waves and face electrodes to measure eye muscle activity, and then put them to bed in a quiet, dark room.

The subjects were woken at various intervals – some during REM sleep, some during non-REM sleep – and asked if they could report a dream. The results were dramatic. In 80 per cent of the awakenings during REM sleep dreams could be reported, but during NREM sleep that figure was just 6 per cent. Intriguingly, the researchers even noted some correlation between the direction of the dreamer's eye movements during REM sleep and the nature of the dream. The one participant who was detected having side-to-side eye movements reported a dream about watching two people throw tomatoes at each other!

Why do we like scary movies?

The enduring popularity of frightening horror and thriller movies poses a psychological paradox: the scarier the film, the more people like it. Other popular forms of scary entertainment include haunted-house shows, ghost trains and alarming roller coasters. Within these types of entertainment there is a diversity of experiences on offer, from creeping dread to sudden shocks, and from thrilling excitement to horrified disgust, so there might not be a simple answer to the question (studies of horror films, for instance, have run into trouble by focusing solely on, say, slasher movies, and excluding psychological horror). But there is clearly a widespread phenomenon at work here; can psychology explain it?

Fear factors

One of the first things to note about scary movies and the emotion in which they trade is that fear is one of the most universal emotions, with a high degree of cross-cultural correspondence between influencing factors. For instance, a Western movie viewer might find a Korean comedy incomprehensible because of its reliance on alien socio-cultural tropes, but will almost effortlessly recognize and respond to a Korean horror movie. The common culture of fear probably reflects the evolutionary origins of innate emotional responses. A 2010 study by Nobuo Masataka and others demonstrated the effects of what is known as 'prepared learning', showing that children as young as three, from an urban culture, spot snakes in an image presented on a screen much faster than they spot flowers, and respond even more quickly when the snakes shown are poised to strike.

The evolutionary roots of such a response are obvious – atavistic fear of predation. Other common elements of our fear response, such as fear of contagion and fear of personal violation, probably have equally straightforward evolutionary origins. In 2004 Hank Davis and Andrea Javor at the University of Guelph asked their study participants to rate forty horror films according to these three themes (predation, contagion and personal violation), and found a strong correlation between the box-office success of the films and high scores in these categories. In other words, the most successful films really are those that best tap into our most primal fears, or what Davis calls 'our evolved cognitive machinery'.

Lure of the id

This may explain why such movies are scary, but not why people enjoy an ostensibly unpleasant experience. Freud's influential essay on 'The Uncanny' (1919) engendered a rich tradition of psychodynamic explanations (those that draw on the psychodynamic philosophy of psychology, which grew out of the psychoanalysis of Freud, Jung and others – *see* page 37). In the Freudian tradition, horror resurrects long-buried emotions and forbidden desires, offering the vicarious thrill of a dip into the id. Meanwhile, for Jungians the appeal of scary stories is that of communing with archetypes – primordial cultural templates deeply embedded in the collective psyche, which trigger profound emotional resonance.

The theories of Freud and Jung are regarded by the wider psychology community as philosophies rather than testable scientific hypotheses. More recent attempts to explain the appeal of scary movies have included Dolf Zillmann's 'excitation-transfer' hypothesis from the 1970s. Zillmann suggested that horror audiences feel good at the end of a movie, when tension has been relieved and good has triumphed, in a modern version of the ancient Greek notion of catharsis. The obvious flaw in this theory is that in many horror films there is no upbeat resolution.

Another theory is that scary movies fulfil a similar function to that sometimes attributed to dreams: as a kind of virtual-reality rehearsal for coping with threat scenarios from real life. By experiencing fear in a fictional universe, we can prepare to deal with it in the real world.

The snuggle effect

In 1986, Zillmann, Norbert Mundorf and others published a study showing that male undergraduates enjoyed a scary movie more if their female viewing partner showed distress, while female students enjoyed it more if their male viewing partners remained stoic and unruffled. A classic study from the 1960s showed that men who met a young woman in a fear-provoking situation on an unsteady suspension bridge were more attracted to her than those who met her on stable ground, suggesting a misattribution effect that can arise when heightened arousal (in the physiological, adrenaline-pumping sense) is transferred into feelings of sexual attraction.

Perhaps something similar is at work when couples go to scary movies, in what has been labelled the 'snuggle effect'. It may even be that the combination of the heightened response aroused by a scary film, with the safe, controlled environment of watching a fictional movie, makes possible a kind of meta-emotion, in which the viewer is able to observe and delight in his or her own fear response.

Can you tell the difference between hot and cold water?

One of the simplest yet most striking demonstrations in psychophysics (the branch of psychology that uses carefully measured stimuli to study perception) shows that it is not always possible to tell the difference between hot and cold water. This simple experiment can be performed by anyone, and is especially good fun for kids. All you need is three large bowls, basins or buckets. Fill one with cold water, one with warm water and one with hot water, and arrange them in a row in that order. Put one hand in the cold water and the other in the hot water, and wait for a minute or two until the sensations of coolness and heat have subsided. Now plunge both hands into the middle bucket of warm water and describe what each hand feels.

Habituation

The hand that was in the cold water will feel hot, while the hand that was in hot water will feel cold, yet both are sensing water of the same temperature. This apparent paradox is the result of a phenomenon called 'habituation' or 'adaptation', in which continued or repeated exposure to a stimulus causes the response to diminish. For instance, if someone touches you unexpectedly on the wrist you might jump, but you quickly stop sensing the pressure of your watch strap on the same wrist. Habituation can result when the nerve cells get exhausted from continually firing, so they stop sending signals to the brain.

Paradoxical responses

Habituation is not the only way to experience a temperature sensation paradox. Other such paradoxes arise from the arrangement of temperature-sensing nerve endings in your skin. The receptors that sense temperature (known as thermoreceptors) are found near the outer layers of skin, in the outermost 0.6 mm ($\frac{1}{50}$ in), and come in two kinds: cold and warm receptors. When a cold receptor fires, you register a sensation of coolness from that point, and when a warm receptor fires you get a sensation of warmness. Because the sensors are spaced apart and not paired up, if you apply a warm probe to a patch of skin that has only a cold receptor, firing of the receptor may be triggered, resulting in the sensation of coldness even though the probe was warm: this is a paradoxical response.

The mystery of hot

One psychophysical mystery is how we can sense hot when we have only cold and warm thermoreceptors. Warm thermoreceptors respond most strongly around body temperature but will also respond to higher temperatures, while cold receptors respond to both cold and hot stimuli. One theory is that the sensation of heat results when both warm and cold thermoreceptors are triggered at the same time, and this is supported by an apparatus called a heat grill, which again fools the body's systems of temperature perception. In a heat grill, warm and cold water are passed through coils of copper tubing that interlace in the centre. At each end the coil is either warm or cold only, so if you grasp each end you can tell the difference, but if you grasp the centre, warm and cold stimuli are simultaneously presented to your hands, resulting in the sensation of hot. Some people will even draw away as though they have been burnt.

Cold fever

Yet another paradoxical temperature perception occurs during a fever, when you get shivering cold despite having an elevated core temperature. Temperature sensation takes place in the outer layers of the skin, and hence depends on both the external temperature and the flow of blood to the outer skin. It may be that when you have a fever, resources need to be diverted to internal organs and systems, and hence blood is directed away from the outer skin, which is cooler as a result – hence both the paradoxical sensation of cold and the pale colouration that sometimes accompanies fever. The peripheral location of thermoreceptors also means that people exposed to microwave radiation, which causes internal heating, can be getting cooked without even feeling it.

Are you a left-brained or a right-brained person?

One of the most common myths about the brain, ranking alongside the canard that we use only 10 per cent of our brains, is that you can be a left- or right-brained person. According to this myth, your personality and 'cognitive style' are determined by which side of your brain is dominant, and the sides themselves have broadly different areas of functionality. The left brain is said to be analytical and verbal, while the right brain is creative and emotional. Where did this myth come from, and how much truth is there in it?

The hemispheres

Firstly it is necessary to explain what is meant by left and right brains. This is a reference to the cerebral

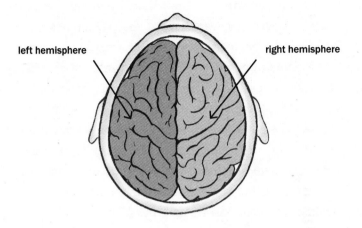

left hemisphere   right hemisphere

hemispheres, which are the bits you see when you look at a picture of a brain.

The hemispheres make up the cerebral cortex, the largest, outermost parts of the brain, with a big trench or fissure separating the two sides. Normally these hemispheres are connected by bands or bridges of nerve fibres, most notably one called the corpus callosum, a thick band of over 600 million nerve fibres. This allows them to communicate and work in tandem, as does the fact that perceptual information from the external world feeds into both of them at the same time, so the two hemispheres usually get the same input.

Scientists naturally wondered what would happen if the corpus callosum was severed to produce so-called 'split brains', and in the 1960s Roger Sperry (who would eventually win a Nobel prize for his work) started experimenting with split-brain cats. Eventually he and Michael Gazzaniga were invited to test humans who had their corpus callosum bridges surgically severed to alleviate crippling epilepsy, and an influential series of studies resulted. These split-brain experiments showed that there are indeed differences in what each hemisphere can do, most notably finding that in most patients the right hemisphere struggled to produce speech. The findings of the experiments were nuanced and complex, but this was inevitably obscured in the popular science reporting that they inspired.

Birth of a myth

In 1973 the *New York Times Magazine* published an article titled, 'We Are Left-Brained or Right-Brained', which began: 'Two very different persons inhabit our heads ... One of them is verbal, analytic, dominant. The other is artistic ... ' This was followed by similar articles in *Time*, the *Harvard Business Review* and *Psychology Today*. A popular scientific myth was born, and left and right brain have now become shorthand for the broadest of generalizations about cognitive style. The left brain is a clever but boring accountant on the autistic spectrum, while the right brain is dim-witted but free spirited, emotional and creative. Sperry himself had warned, 'experimentally observed polarity in right–left cognitive style is an idea in general with which it is very easy to run wild', but even he could hardly have expected just how wild it would run!

Ever since, psychologists have been pointing out the fallacies of the popular left- and right-brain generalization. In 2013 definitive evidence emerged in the shape of a study by neuroscientists at the University of Utah, who scanned the brains of more than a thousand people, concluding: 'Lateralization of brain connections appears to be a local rather than global property of brain networks, and our data are not consistent with a whole-brain phenotype of greater "left-brained" or greater "right-brained" network strength across individuals.' In other words, some particular tasks are associated with heightened activity in specific small areas of the brain, but there is no evidence that in some people one hemisphere is dominant over the other.

Top and bottom?

In summary, says leading cognitive neuroscientist Kara D. Federmeier, 'it seems safe to say that for the most part we all use both sides of our brains almost all the time'. In split-brain patients, there are indeed areas of difference, but even these are not clear-cut. So while the right hemisphere struggles to speak, it is nonetheless involved in processing some aspects of language, such as intonation and emphasis. Meanwhile, in contrast to the popular conception that the right hemisphere is creative while the left is somehow unimaginative, Gazzaniga's conclusion from the split-brain experiments was that the left hemisphere is the seat of 'creative, narrative talent'.

Perhaps it would be more helpful to break away from the left- and right-brain distinction. In a book written with Wayne Miller, *Top Brain, Bottom Brain: Surprising Insights into How You Think* (2014), leading cognitive psychologist Stephen Kosslyn proposes an alternative paradigm to left and right brain, emphasizing instead the 'top and bottom parts. Among other things, the top part sets up plans and revises those plans when expected events do not occur; the bottom classifies and interprets what we perceive.'

Are there two different people in your head?

Extraordinary and counter-intuitive though it may sound, there is evidence that your mind is composed of two distinct consciousnesses. One of the most intriguing findings of the split-brain experiments of Roger Sperry and Michael Gazzaniga (*see* page 63) was that each of a person's hemispheres can be fed different information, leading to different thoughts in each hemisphere – and that each will be unaware of what the other half is thinking! 'After many years of fascinating research on the split brain, it appears that the . . . left hemisphere has a conscious experience very different from that of the . . . right brain,' Gazzaniga reflected in 2002.

Competing hemispheres

The key experimental method in the split-brain studies involved presenting each of a person's cerebral hemispheres with a different picture. Each eye connects to both hemispheres, so you cannot simply show a different picture to each eye, but in each eye the left visual field (that is, the left half of what the eye sees) feeds into the right hemisphere, and the right visual field to the left hemisphere. By flashing pictures split down the middle for just a moment, the experimenters prevented the subject moving his or her eyes, ensuring that each hemisphere did indeed get a different input. The results were fascinating.

A split-brain patient could easily describe pictures seen in his right visual field (processed only by the left hemisphere), but seemed unable to say what the right hemisphere had seen. However, he was able to pick out the correct reference photo with his left hand, which is 'under the control' of the right hemisphere. In other words, it is possible for the right hemisphere to know something that the left hemisphere does not.

Equally dramatic results occurred when the split-brain subject was given a task involving both hands. Cognitive neuroscientist Kara D. Federmeier, a researcher into hemispheric asymmetries, notes that 'patients' hands – one controlled by each hemisphere – literally fought for control of a particular task; it is intriguing to imagine that kind of struggle routinely taking place internally for everyone else!' In other words, competing consciousnesses could be a feature of normal human psychology.

The bicameral mind

One extraordinary hypothesis that developed from this kind of thinking is Julian Jaynes' theory in his 1976 book *The Origin of Consciousness in the Breakdown of the Bicameral Mind* (where bicameral means 'two-chambered'). Jaynes argued that ancient humans' consciousness was partitioned, so that for most of human evolution the consciousness embodied in the right hemisphere was not accessible to that in the left hemisphere. Prehistoric humans encountered this 'right-brain' consciousness through auditory and other hallucinations – in other words, voices in the head similar to those experienced by schizophrenics. These may have been interpreted as messages from supernatural entities, such as gods, ancestors or personal spirit guides (such as the Ancient Egyptian *ka* or the Graeco-Roman *genius*). Only when humans developed a metaphorical language to describe and process their own thinking and right-brain consciousness became integrated into the whole – that is, around the end of the Bronze Age and the start of the Iron Age (*c.* 1200 BCE in the Near East) – did consciousness in the modern sense arise.

Jaynes's theory is not widely supported, but raises issues for both ancient history and modern psychology. Do the voices heard by psychotics derive from the right hemisphere, which has somehow become 'unmoored' or decoupled from the left? In the healthy and mentally ill alike, what is the nature of consciousness in the light of what neuroscientists call the laterality of the brain (i.e. the division of cognitive processing between the hemispheres)? Gazzaniga believes that 'the inventive and interpreting left hemisphere has a conscious experience very different from that of the truthful, literal right brain. Although both hemispheres can be viewed as conscious, the left brain's consciousness far surpasses that of the right.' But might the left brain's consciousness also be different, and even to some degree separate from that of the right?

The interpreter

In one split-brain experiment, the right hemisphere was shown a snowy scene while the left was shown a chicken's claw, and the subject was asked to pick cards that matched what he had seen. With his right hand he picked a card showing a chicken, while his left hand picked a card showing a snow shovel. When asked to explain the discrepancy, the subject's left brain demonstrated a mind module that Gazzaniga labelled 'the interpreter', which tries to stitch together a story to fit the facts. In this case the subject volunteered that the shovel was needed to clear up after the chicken. It is this 'interpreter' function that Gazzaniga described as 'the creative, narrative talent', explaining that findings such as these:

> . . . suggest that the interpretive mechanism of the left hemisphere is always hard at work, seeking the meaning of events. It is constantly looking for order and reason, even when there is none – which leads it continually to make mistakes. It tends to overgeneralize, frequently constructing a potential past as opposed to a true one.

Is it a duck
or a rabbit?

The duck-rabbit is a classic example of a type of visual illusion known as an ambiguous figure. It can be interpreted as either a duck or a rabbit, and you can 'flip' between interpretations within seconds.

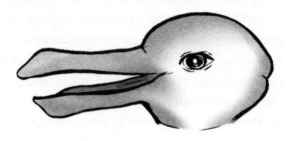

Just an illusion

Ambiguous figures are part of a class of illusions known as illusions of cognition. Other widely known ambiguous figures are the young woman-old crone and the Necker cube, a wire-framed cube that can be seen either as projecting out at the viewer or receding. Illusions of cognition such as these arise from mental processes, rather than the physical properties of the body or external world.

There are many other types of illusion, ranging from optical illusions – which result from optical properties of a phenomenon and don't depend on properties of human perception, such as when a pencil in a glass of water looks crooked – to illusions caused by the physiology of the human eye. For instance, if you stare at a red square for thirty seconds and then transfer your gaze to a white surface you will see a ghostly green square. This results from retinal fatigue, which is where the nerve cells in the retina responsible for perceiving the colour red get tired, so that when you look at the white surface they are no longer firing; your brain then perceives the absence of red signals as absence of red, subtracting red and leaving green. These physiological types of illusion stem from processes at the 'bottom' of the visual system, while ambiguous figures result from the cognitive top of the system, showing top-down processing at work.

Gestalt

Illusions of all sorts are of interest to psychologists because of what they reveal about the neurophysiology and psychology of perception. Ambiguous figures, for instance, demonstrate how perception can be a constructive process, in which the mind starts with a perceptual framework into which incoming stimulus is fitted. The way in which the figure can 'flip' between states shows how images are often perceived as a 'whole', known in psychology by the German term '*gestalt*'. Rather than attending to the components that make up the image, it is perceived all at once.

Müller-Lyer

One of the simplest illusions seems to depend on a highly complex explanation. Look at the horizontal lines between the arrowheads below:

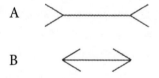

Which is longer, the horizontal line in A or the one in B? In fact the two lines are of identical length, but the illusion that A is longer persists even when you know this. This is known as the Müller-Lyer illusion after the German psychologist who first described it. Richard Gregory explained the illusion as an example of top-down processing, demonstrating how conscious perception is a construct that only partly depends on reality. The diagonal lines act as perceptual cues – Gregory says they look like either the near or far corner of a room or building – and this in turn suggests that the line in the far corner, being further away, must be longer in reality in order to appear the same length as the near one. Your brain therefore imposes this inferred information onto your perception of the line, and there's nothing you can do about it.

One piece of evidence that backs up Gregory's explanation is the finding that the illusion only works on people from cultures with artefacts featuring straight edges and right angles – so-called carpentered worlds. People from non-carpentered worlds, such as the San of sub-Saharan Africa, do not fall for the illusion, perhaps because they have not absorbed the rules of linear perspective in the way we have.

Did you see that gorilla?

Would you notice a man in a gorilla suit walking across a basketball court in the middle of a game? Incredibly, around half the participants in a well-known psychology experiment failed to notice just this, because they had been asked to count passes between specific players. Their attention was focused on a specific task, so the gorilla was invisible.

Attention at the centre

The invisible gorilla is one of the more remarkable findings from a fruitful and significant area of study in psychology: the topic of attention. 'Everyone knows what attention is,' wrote William James in 1890. 'It is the taking possession by the mind in clear and vivid form, of one out of what seem several simultaneously possible objects or trains of thought ... It implies withdrawal from some things in order to deal effectively with others.'

Attention is important to psychologists because it is a core mental process, and provides a basis on which to study other mental processes; especially learning. '[Only] when a person is actively engaged in voluntary attention,' note Stephen Porges and Georgia DiGangi in a 1990 paper, 'can functional purposeful activity and learning occur.' Attention may be even more important than this, offering a way to study the central but most elusive concept in psychology – consciousness. Writing in 1980 in *Cognitive Psychology: New Directions*, Alan Allport said that 'hard-nosed information-processing psychologists use attention as a code name for consciousness'. Focal attention – that which we are currently paying attention to and lies at the centre of our awareness – is what Freud meant by 'the conscious'.

A brief history of cognitive psychology

Attention is one of the core concerns of the discipline known as cognitive psychology, which is the psychology of mental processes. In behaviourism, the mind is seen almost as a black box – an impenetrable and unknowable (and ultimately irrelevant) device, the mechanisms of which are irretrievably obscure to science – and psychology should restrict itself to studying only the inputs to (stimuli) and outputs from (behaviour) said box. Cognitive psychology rejects this, and takes as its province precisely the terra incognita of the behaviourists, seeking to explore and investigate the processes of the black box of the mind. In order to do this, however, it relies very heavily on the information-processing approach, which sees the mind as an information-processing system analogous to a computer.

Cognitive psychology had antecedents in the work of Jean Piaget (*see* page 82), but it needed the new soil of information and computer science in order to take root. In 1948 Norbert Wiener published the seminal work *Cybernetics: or Control and Communication in the Animal and the Machine*, introducing to psychology terms such as input and output. That same year, Edward Tolman's classic experiment on rats' learning mazes showed that animals could have internal representations of behaviour, with what he called 'cognitive maps'. George Miller's 1956 paper on the capacity of short-term or working memory, 'The Magical Number 7 Plus or Minus 2', is generally credited as the birth of cognitive psychology, although the discipline did not officially begin until Ulric Neisser's 1967 book *Cognitive Psychology*.

Invisible clowns

To get back to the invisible gorilla, the failure to spot something apparently unmissable is attributed to a phenomenon known as 'inattentional blindness'. When the channels for conscious perception are otherwise occupied, things that fall outside those channels go unnoticed. Inattentional blindness has been demonstrated with such examples as people opening umbrellas, ghosts in a movie theatre and unicycling clowns. In a follow-up version of the original invisible gorilla experiment, forewarned subjects noticed the gorilla but failed to spot a curtain in the background that changed colour.

Where does language come from?

Some of the earliest experiments in psychology concerned the phylogeny of language, which is to say, how human languages developed over the aeons. In their search for the original (in biblical terms, Adamic) language of humanity, several rulers throughout history have been linked to stories of highly unethical experiments in which they had children raised in isolation, or with only deaf mutes for carers, in order to see what language they would speak (*see* opposite).

The language miracle

Such experiments are not only cruel but also lack scientific validity. Modern linguistic scholars use clever language comparisons to reconstruct language lineages and even guess at earlier 'proto' forms of language, such as proto-Indo-European. Of far greater interest to psychologists is the ontogeny of language: the question

Raised without language

According to Herodotus *c.* 429 BCE, the Egyptian Pharaoh Psammetichus found that two children brought up without any linguistic input used the Phrygian word for bread, while the Mogul emperor Akbar the Great (1542–1605) observed that children put in the care of deaf mute nurses had developed sign language. A similar tale is told of the Holy Roman Emperor Frederick II (1194–1250), while in 1493, according to the historian Robert Lindsay of Pitscottie, King James IV of Scotland had two infants and a deaf mute nurse transported to the isolated island of Inchkeith, in the middle of the Firth of Forth. Lindsay wrote, 'Some say they spoke good Hebrew; for my part I know not, but from report', although as the novelist Sir Walter Scott later observed, 'It is more likely they would scream like their dumb nurse, or bleat like the goats and sheep on the island.' In natural experiments where children have apparently grown up without any human contact, as with so-called feral children raised by wolves and such like, the children in fact display no language.

of how children learn to master language so quickly and apparently effortlessly. Newborns can recognize speech patterns heard in the womb, while within the first year infants learn to use cues such as syllable stress to break up a stream of speech into words. By three, most children can use what the American linguist Noam Chomsky in the 1950s called 'generative grammar' – language rules that make it possible to understand and produce (generate) entirely novel sentences.

Chomsky's LAD

The challenge of explaining this extraordinary human language phenomenon, apparently without parallel in the animal world, has led to various theories. The cognitive theory of developmental psychologist Jean Piaget sees language acquisition as part of general learning, with children developing new concepts and learning the verbal labels for them, but this theory does not really address the acquisition of grammar. The behaviourist B. F. Skinner argued that this acquisition was entirely learned through imitation, repetition and reinforcement, but Noam Chomsky responded that the language to which infants are exposed is hopelessly inadequate for learning grammar. Accordingly, in the 1960s Chomsky proposed that humans are born with a mental structure known as the 'language acquisition device' (LAD), which encodes an innate 'Universal Grammar'.

Though Chomsky's LAD theory has been extremely influential, many of his assumptions have since been disproved or at least undermined. It has become apparent that the input to which infants are exposed is much richer than he claimed, and that infants are highly sensitive to the sort of cues (such as prosody and syntax) that they need in order to use a general learning mechanism to bootstrap from parental input to working grammar.

Can you think about something without words?

The philosopher Ludwig Wittgenstein famously wrote, 'The limits of my language mean the limits of my world' (*Tractatus Logico-Philosophicus*, 1922), suggesting the conceptual universe is bounded by language. Thinking about thinking seems impossible without words, but is thought itself really inextricably bound up with language? Without a word for something can we have a concept of it? A strong school in psychology has argued, following Wittgenstein, that thought is dependent upon, or even solely caused by, language; a view known as 'linguistic determinism' (as in, cognition is determined by language).

Twenty words for snow

The most influential advocates of this view are linguist Benjamin Lee Whorf, and linguist and anthropologist Edward Sapir. The Sapir-Whorf (aka Whorfian) theory, known as the 'linguistic relativity hypothesis', holds that concepts are determined by the words that are used for them, and therefore that the understanding and perception of the world experienced by each culture or individual can only be understood relative to their language (hence linguistic relativity). Their hypothesis developed in the 1920s and 1930s from their observations of striking differences between what they called Standard Average European (SAE) languages and more exotic languages such as Hopi and Inuit. Whorf claimed that Hopi, for instance, makes no linguistic distinction between past, present and future, while the Inuit, he famously claimed, have twenty different words for snow. Accordingly, claims the Sapir-Whorf hypothesis, the Inuit literally perceive more varieties of snow than SAE speakers, whose perceptual categories are circumscribed by having just one or two words for snow.

This classic illustration of linguistic relativity has since been heavily challenged; for instance, Whorf may have exaggerated the number of Inuit words for snow. Another criticism of linguistic relativity is that, were it categorically true, it would not be possible to translate from, say, Hopi to SAE, which is not the case.

The colour challenge

Colour perception and description has been used as a readily available means of testing the predictions of linguistic determinism. Many languages around the world recognize fewer basic or focal colour categories than English, which has words for all eleven. For instance, according to a 1954 study, the Dani of New Guinea only had two words for colours (*mola* meaning bright, warm colours and *mili* meaning dark, cold ones). Intriguing research by Berlin and Kay in 1969 found that words for focal colours always occur in a hierarchy: if only two terms are used they apply to black and white, the third term will be red, the fourth and fifth green and yellow, and so on, with purple, pink and orange only used if all the others are also present.

More significantly for linguistic determinism, there is strong evidence that despite the constraints of language, 'colour-term poor' speakers can recognize all the focal colours, and that the main influence on colour perception is the physiology of the visual system. So colour perception turns out to have strong similarities across cultures, irrespective of language, which undermines the determinist view.

Curare for the curious

The Sapir-Whorf hypothesis is not the only theory arguing that language determines thought. The early behaviourist John B. Watson proposed an extreme view that thinking is talking, and that what we think are internal thought processes are actually inaudible 'subvocalizations', or tiny vibrations of the vocal cords. In other words, if we can't talk, we can't think. Known as 'peripheralism', Watson's theory was plausible when proposed in 1912, because the technology was not available to determine whether such subvocalizations occurred, but in 1947 a dramatic experiment by E. M. Smith and others demolished it. Smith injected himself with curare, a paralytic poison that stops all skeletal muscle contractions. Kept alive only by an artificial lung that breathed for him, he was also unable to move his vocal cords, but continued to have thoughts and perceptions nonetheless.

Why do we forget?

Forgetting seems like one of the worst defects of the human organism. This is particularly true given that the capacity of the human memory is estimated at around 2.5 petabytes of information (2.5 million gigabytes) – equivalent to three million hours (*c.* 340 years) of TV recordings on a digital video recorder. If memories are stored in the form of connections between neurons, then the total number of memories it would be theoretically possible to store could be greater than the number of atoms in the universe.

Given this apparently colossal capacity, why should we have to forget anything at all? Wouldn't it be nice to have total recall, like a computer or the Internet? No more lost keys or missed anniversaries, just to take some of the more trivial consequences of forgetting.

The leading theory to explain the utility of forgetting is based on the psychological phenomena of 'interference' and 'decay'. Interference is where one memory interferes with the recall of another. You might struggle to remember a name you heard this morning simply because you met three other people since. Decay is the process by which information fades if it is not laid down as a memory, for whatever reason. To understand this better, we need to look at the model of memory as it is understood in cognitive psychology.

How are memories made?

The question of how memories are made is one of the principal concerns of psychology, articulated as early as 1890 by William James in his classic work, *The Principles of Psychology*:

> The stream of thought flows on; but most of its segments fall into the bottomless abyss of oblivion. Of some, no memory survives the instant of their passage. Of others, it is confined to a few moments, hours, or days. Others, again, leave vestiges which are indestructible, and by means of which they may be recalled as long as life endures. Can we explain these differences?

Memory is generally understood to consist of two major components: short- and long-term memory. A constant river of information from your senses (or from your imagination) arrives in your brain and is held in a sensory register, where attention (*see* page 76) acts as a filter to select only the most important or noticeable bits for consideration in 'short-term memory', also known as 'working memory'. Information in your working memory can be used immediately, or, again depending on its importance or notability, encoded into 'long-term memory'. Here it can be stored for later retrieval. The encoding process is the crucial step that determines whether an event, fact or feeling falls 'into the bottomless abyss of oblivion' or leaves 'vestiges which are indestructible'.

Sea slugs and the secret of the engram

The physiology corresponding to this model of memory formation is an area of controversy, with the physical trace of a memory, sometimes known as the 'engram', often the object of abuse by charlatans and quacks. But some clues have emerged from the Nobel prize-winning work of American-Austrian neuropsychiatrist Eric Kandel, who used the sea slug as an animal model for human memory formation. The sea slug, or sea hare, has a relatively simple system of just 20,000 neurons; some large enough to be visible to the naked eye. Kandel and colleagues were able to show that a short-term memory is formed when a synapse – the connection between nerve cells, by which they signal each other – is strengthened, so that the signal between two nerve cells is amplified. Meanwhile, a long-term memory involves major changes to the structure of synapses, effectively resulting in the formation of a new synapse.

Forget to remember

'Encoding', or 'memory formation', is only one side of the process required for remembering; the other side of the coin is 'recall', or retrieval of the encoded memory. Interference makes recall harder, so efficient recall of important memories (such as those that assist survival) must require some degree of selective memory. How to ensure that memory is selective, and that only the most useful and important memories are encoded? This is where decay comes in: information in short-term memory decays, unless it is reinforced through rehearsal or attention. So you will only encode a memory for the rock under which the poisonous snake lives, rather than every rock you ever saw, which in turn means that when you need to recall which rock conceals danger, your recall is not interfered with by the other 'rock' memories. It may be necessary to forget some things in order to better remember more important things.

Can a machine think?

In 1950, the English mathematician and computer-science pioneer Alan Turing wrote an article responding to the question, 'Can a machine be intelligent?' His immediate answer was that the question is 'too meaningless to deserve discussion'.

The Turing test

Instead, Turing proposed a test of whether a machine could appear to be intelligent: the 'imitation game', now known as the 'Turing test'. Turing argued that if a machine, conversing via answers written on a screen, could fool a human into thinking that he or she is talking to another human, then the machine would have to be considered intelligent. Passing the Turing test – a milestone that Turing predicted would be achieved by 2000 – has been one of the primary goals of the field of artificial intelligence (AI), the discipline sitting at the junction of cognitive psychology and computer science.

Rise of the machines

Artificial intelligence grew out of the work of Turing and others in the brave new world of computers. After the Second World War, Turing helped to develop the world's first electronic digital computer, but he tragically committed suicide in 1954, two years before the first AI computer program arrived. In 1956 American researchers Allen Newell, J. C. Shaw and Herbert Simon introduced 'Logic Theorist': an AI that proved able to determine for itself the basic equations of logic, even coming up with a better proof than that already known. That same year, a conference at Dartmouth College, in Hanover, New Hampshire, saw the term 'AI' coined, and the field formally came into being.

The success of Logic Theorist prompted wildly optimistic predictions about the imminent rise of AI. Allen Newell predicted that 'Within ten years a digital computer will be the world's chess champion, unless the rules bar it from competition', while MIT cognitive scientist Marvin Minsky proclaimed, 'Within a generation . . . the problem of creating "artificial intelligence" will substantially be solved.'

Rapid advances in computer technology did nothing to dent the confidence of AI researchers, and by the 1960s the scientist Herbert Simon predicted that AI would overtake human intelligence within twenty years.

Exponentially increasing computer power could be harnessed to run programs of increasing complexity, and intelligence would emerge. This approach, sometimes known as 'Good Old Fashioned AI', focused initially on challenges such as beating human grandmasters at chess, but it took until 1997 before this feat was finally accomplished, when IBM's 'Deep Blue' supercomputer defeated world champion Garry Kasparov. In 2011, IBM's 'Watson' AI defeated human champions on the game show *Jeopardy!*, but many of the grand predictions for AI have gone unfulfilled.

In 2014 Turing's prediction regarding his test seemed finally to have been met (albeit over a decade late), when a chatbot named 'Eugene Goostman' was said to have passed the test. However, this claim is controversial because the chatbot fooled only a third of the judges, and has been criticized for 'gaming' the test by posing as a thirteen-year-old Ukrainian with shaky English.

The Chinese Room

Even if an AI can pass the Turing test, does this mean it can think? One major objection to the claim is that passing the test is no guarantee that an AI had achieved 'symbol grounding'; the ability to know what symbols, words or concepts really 'mean'. In the early 1980s, the philosopher John Searle proposed a thought experiment called the 'Chinese Room' to illustrate this point. Imagine a man in a sealed room, to whom written questions are passed through a slot. The questions are in Chinese, which the man cannot understand, but he has a giant book of syntactical and semantic rules that allows him to process the questions and write answers in Chinese. To the people receiving his response, it would appear that he can understand Chinese, but in fact he has no such comprehension.

This is just one of the tough – and potentially unresolvable – issues facing AI and the wider field of the study of consciousness; elements of what is sometimes called the 'hard problem' of consciousness. A related issue is whether desires, emotions or intentions 'programmed' into AIs mean the same as our desires and intentions. For instance, consider a thermostat, a device with electrical properties that change in response to changing temperature, such that it turns the heating up or down to keep the temperature at a set level. Does the thermostat 'want' to keep your living room at a toasty 21°C (70°F)? It may sound crazy to claim that it does, but if we cannot give a clear definition of what it means to 'want' something, who is to say otherwise?

Why do nice guys finish last?

The phrase 'nice guys finish last' is attributed to hard-nosed baseball manager Leo Durocher in 1946. Since then it has come to encapsulate a set of assumptions about temperament, masculinity and interpersonal relations. What does psychology tell us about these assumptions? Is there evidence that nice guys really do finish last, in love, life or lucre?

The Big Five

What do we mean by 'nice'? In personality terms, the relevant characteristic – or 'dimension' – is agreeableness. Agreeableness includes traits such as being co-operative, warm, kind and non-argumentative. It is one of the 'Big Five personality dimensions' or factors, alongside openness, extraversion–introversion, neuroticism and conscientiousness. These are sometimes called dimensions because each one describes a spectrum, with individuals falling somewhere along that spectrum.

These dimensions are known as the Big Five because

statistical analysis of a huge range of different personality traits or factors show that they all boil down to
these five. For instance, creativity, sophistication and
curiosity all sound like different traits, but analysis
shows that an individual's scores on tests of these
factors correlate closely together, and that across
a group of people they tend to vary together. This
suggests that a single factor underlies all of these traits,
and psychologists who study personality refer to it
as openness, aka culture, or openness to experience.
People at one end of this dimension are close-
minded, uninquisitive, less creative and less analytical,
while those at the other end are highly analytical,
sophisticated and creative, and embrace novelty. The
agreeableness dimension has traits such as warmth,
generosity, altruism and compliance at one end, with
coldness, meanness, argumentativeness, selfishness and
tough-mindedness at the other.

There are many other ways of grouping together and
breaking down personality traits, and arguments in
favour of even fewer than five basic traits. Influential
German psychologist of personality and individual
differences Hans Eysenck (1916–97) argues that
conscientiousness and agreeableness are simply facets
of the same underlying personality dimension, which
he terms 'psychoticism', while other research suggests
that there are basically only two axes of personality:
extraversion–introversion and neuroticism–stability.

(For more on personality psychology and the key dimension of extraversion–introversion, see 'Why are some folk shy?', page 146).

Nice Todd vs Jerky Todd

Evidence from studies such as the one by Livingston and others (*see* opposite) suggest that there really is some truth to the saying 'nice guys finish last' when it comes to careers and remuneration. On the romantic side, the picture is more complicated. A 2003 study asked women to rate dating profiles identical except for a few key traits, and found that women were far more likely to say they would date 'Nice Todd' than 'Jerky Todd'. This agrees with other studies showing that women rate 'nice' qualities as more attractive for long-term partnership, but on the downside qualities such as 'niceness' come with baggage: associated qualities and assumptions, such as that nice men are likely to be less assertive and less sexually experienced.

It pays to be disagreeable

In 2011, a study by Beth Livingston, Timothy Judge and Charlie Hurst, published in the *Journal of Personality and Social Psychology*, looked at the relationship between agreeableness and salary in 10,000 workers across a variety of professions and ages. They found that men who measured below average on agreeableness earned approximately 18 per cent more than nicer guys, but that this correlation was much weaker for women, with less agreeable women earning 5 per cent more than their agreeable counterparts. The income premium for disagreeableness is more than three times stronger for men than women, and for every standard deviation difference in level of agreeableness (roughly 0.75 points on a 5- or 6-point measurement scale), men reported almost $10,000 less in annual earnings. Livingston and her colleagues conclude: 'For men, it literally pays to be a contrarian ... Nice guys do not necessarily finish last, but they do finish a distant second in terms of earnings.'

Why are people racist?

Racism is a form of prejudice, which is an attitude (usually negative) towards a group, or members of that group, although sometimes a distinction is made between an individual's racial prejudice and a society's political and economic ideology of racism.

Understanding prejudices such as racism has been one of the primary goals of the field known as social psychology, which investigates how and why individuals behave in social situations. The study of prejudice and related issues became a particular focus after the Second World War, with its terrible atrocities based on bigotry, and in the context of civil rights in America and elsewhere from the 1950s.

The roots of racism

Social psychologists have identified three possible explanations for racism: individual personality traits, such as the 'authoritarian personality'; environmental factors, such as pressure to conform to social norms, and conflict between groups stemming from competition; and, thirdly, the effects of social identity, which is to say, the psychological consequences of simply being a member of a group.

The authoritarian personality is a concept proposed by Theodor Adorno and others in 1950, based on their attempts to understand fascism in the wake of the Nazis. Adorno and colleagues developed scales to measure personality variables such as anti-Semitism, conservatism and respect for authority, showing that these traits corresponded with fascistic tendencies. They thus attributed racism to personality traits. Milton Rokeach suggested in 1954 that the key trait here is dogmatism, which applies to right- and left-wing individuals alike.

Classic studies in social psychology gave evidence that external factors can also feed into racism. A 1952 study of black and white coalminers in West Virginia showed that while underground the miners were highly integrated, above ground they were strongly segregated. The inference was that the men were conforming to social norms in the socially constricted above-ground world, but when in the heat and peril of the working environment, cut off from society and its norms, they were able to disregard these.

Ganging up

In 1961 Muzafer Sherif took twenty-two middle-class white children from summer camp, randomly assigned them to two groups and set them against one another in competition. He found that they rapidly developed strong group identities and came into conflict with one another, each cultivating strong antipathies to the other group. Sherif interpreted this as evidence that competition for resources (in this case, prizes awarded in a sporting tournament) is the root of intergroup conflict and hence prejudice.

In 1971 Henri Tajfel extended Sherif's paradigm of randomly assigned groups to investigate the minimal conditions necessary for formation of group identity: this was known as the 'minimal group paradigm'. He asked a group of teenage boys to express preferences for slides of paintings by abstract painters Paul Klee and Wassily Kandinsky, then randomly assigned them to groups of those names. Each boy, working individually, then had to allocate points (exchangeable for negligible monetary rewards) to fellow group members (ingroup) or members of the other group (outgroup).

Tajfel found that the boys showed very strong ingroup favouritism and disfavoured the outgroup, even though the basis for the grouping was utterly superficial and they had no contact with nor knew anything about either in- or outgroup members. The favouritism persisted even when the boys were told that the group assignment was completely random.

The in crowd

Tajfel's conclusion was that simply being a member of a group automatically triggers a set of attitudes, based on what he called social identity theory. This is the theory that individuals derive part of their identity from social groups to which they belong, and that in order to maximize their positive self-image they manufacture a positive image of their group, partly by comparing outgroups unfavourably with their ingroup. Thus white people might boost their self-image by boosting their ethnic group, which in turn is achieved in part by denigrating outgroups of other ethnicities.

Would you buy a used car from this man?

Although it is not clear when willingness to purchase second-hand automobiles was first mentioned as the gold standard for trustworthiness, the trope became culturally embedded after the appearance of a poster showing the thirty-seventh American president Richard Nixon – popularly known as 'Tricky Dicky' on becoming the epitome of the shifty politician – with the caption, 'Would you buy a used car from this man?'

Scientists vs misers

Trustworthiness is one of the key traits on which we judge other people. Evolutionary psychologists, who study the likely origins of and evolutionary rationales for behaviours, point out the self-evident advantages of being able to make such judgements. In survival situations, poor judgements on whether a stranger is trustworthy could be deadly. So what does psychology tell us about how people make this kind of interpersonal judgement?

One early theory about the process of making such judgements – known as 'social cognition' – was that each of us is like a scientist, collecting and analysing the evidence before making considered and rational assessments. This was criticized as unrealistic, and social psychologists now favour the 'cognitive miser' hypothesis, which assumes that limited resources, including time and mental processing power, mean that we have to be parsimonious and make the most efficient judgements possible, often on the basis of limited information. To achieve this, we use mental rules of thumb, technically known as 'heuristics', which serve as cognitive short cuts. In consequence, we tend to make snap judgements based on generalizations and stereotypes.

Central traits

What kind of heuristics might affect your judgement of the used-car salesman? A classic 1946 study by the American Solomon Asch found that people's perceptions of a character based on a fictional biography were dramatically swayed by one small change. In his experiment, two groups read the exact same biography and then chose adjectives that fitted the fictional person, but for one group the person was described as 'warm', and for the other, 'cold'. Based on this difference, the person was seen either as generous, sociable and humorous, or the exact opposite. Asch called the warm–cold dimension a 'central trait', meaning that it strongly influenced the overall impression, as opposed to peripheral traits that had little impact on perceptions and assumptions about other traits. However, the warm–cold trait itself does not appear to influence assessments of reliability and trustworthiness.

So what might? We hold implicit theories about others' personalities, and one characteristic of these implicit personality theories is that they assume that some traits and characteristics cluster together. For instance, physical attractiveness is implicitly associated with other positive attributes, a form of bias known as the 'halo effect' (*see* page 110). Names have been shown to carry implicit baggage, so that people find some names trustworthier than others (for example, in a 1973 study the names David and Karen were shown to be 'trustworthy', while Elmer and Bertha were associated with 'unattractiveness'). But perhaps the most important attribute for judging trustworthiness is a person's face.

All in the face

A range of studies have shown facial attributes dramatically affect judgements of trustworthiness. According to a 2014 study by Carmel Sofer of Princeton University and Radboud University Nijmegen in the Netherlands, having an average face makes you seem more trustworthy, possibly because 'Face typicality likely indicates familiarity and cultural affiliation'.

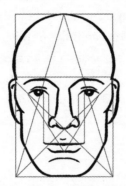

Schematic face showing key facial geometries

Other studies show that people may take as little as 38 milliseconds to make trustworthiness decisions about faces, assessing with extraordinary rapidity facial geometry that is associated with trust. These judgements are probably made by a brain structure called the amygdala. Experiments on patients with brain damage to the amygdala show that such individuals are poor at making judgements of trustworthiness – in fact their assessments tend to be the opposite of the consensus. What's more, a 2014 brain-imaging study showed that these instant judgements are made by your un- or preconscious, without conscious awareness. 'Our findings suggest that the brain automatically responds to a face's trustworthiness before it is even consciously perceived,' according to Dr Jonathan Freeman, an assistant professor in New York University's Department of Psychology. This could account for a well-known phenomenon in social cognition, the 'primacy effect', which is essentially a social psychologist's way of saying that 'first impressions count'.

Why can't bald guys become president?

There have been no bald or balding men elected President of the United States since Eisenhower in 1953, and it is a commonplace of popular political wisdom that a full head of hair is an important, if not essential, electoral asset. When photos suggested Barack Obama might be developing a bald patch during his first term, it was suggested that this might spell doom for his chances of winning a second term. The baldness bar may apply elsewhere too: in the United Kingdom there hasn't been a bald prime minister since Alec Douglas-Home in 1963–4, and even he didn't win the post in an election. Meanwhile, a string of British opposition party leaders, from Neil Kinnock to Michael Howard, were bald and lost elections.

The pattern is not restricted to the top job. In the US in 2008, only 20 per cent of male state governors were bald or balding, along with only around 15 per cent of male senators. Compare this to the general incidence of clinical balding among white Caucasian men (who make up the bulk of elected high officials), which the International Society of Hair Restoration Surgery estimates at 50 per cent in men over forty-five and 60 per cent in those over sixty. Such marked disparity suggests that the baldness bar is a real phenomenon, and not just a statistical artefact or popular misconception.

Halos and horns

Can it be that voters are biased against candidates with little or no hair? How can something as superficial as baldness be such a big factor in what is supposed to be a rational, considered choice based on serious issues and policies? If voter bias is to blame, the obvious explanation is the 'halo effect', a phenomenon named by the psychologist Edward Thorndike to describe a form of cognitive bias in which positive feelings about one attribute are applied to other, unrelated ones. So someone rated as more attractive will also be perceived as more intelligent, more responsible and a better leader, for instance. This has also been called the principle that 'what is beautiful is good'. The opposite of the halo effect is the 'horns effect', where a negative attribute triggers negative bias about other attributes. Assuming that baldness really is a negative attribute, this might cause voters to be biased against bald candidates in their assessment of more relevant attributes.

Bald ambition

Countering this argument are two studies. There is evidence that baldness is correlated with potentially positive perceptions, such as dominance and intelligence. For instance, a 2012 study by the Wharton School of Pennsylvania found that men with shaved heads were perceived as more masculine and dominant, with greater leadership potential. Meanwhile, research by Lee Sigelman and others, published in the *Journal of Nonverbal Behaviour* in 1990, appears to demonstrate that voter bias is not the reason for the under-representation of bald men in high office. In an experimental test of voter bias, they ran simulated congressional races in which the same bald candidates were presented with and without professionally fitted hairpieces.

No voter bias was apparent, suggesting, they pointed out, 'that the link between hair loss and electability may lie in stereotypes of baldness held by power brokers and/or bald and balding men themselves'. In other words, bald men are either inhibited from running successfully (or at all) by their own negative self-concept, or they don't get the financial and other support from donors and party grandees that is so essential for electoral success. Given a level playing field, a bald man might well get elected president.

How can ordinary people commit war crimes?

Horrors like those of the Holocaust posed a massive challenge to psychology: clearly not everyone involved had been a psychotic monster from birth, yet millions were actively engaged or complicit in monstrous crimes. How could this circle be squared?

Psychoanalysing the Nazis

The dark psychology involved is complex and multivariate. The psychology of prejudice, social identity, in- versus outgroup bias and the authoritarian personality are all involved (*see* page 100, 'Why are people racist?', for more on these).

The Asch conformity experiment

Social psychology has been particularly interested in how beliefs, attitudes and behaviours at the level of society affect the individual. In 1951, Solomon Asch devised a test of conformity – the degree to which an individual falls into line with majority – in which the test subject was asked to match a straight line to three comparison lines. It was obvious which of the three comparison lines was the right answer, but Asch tested the subjects in a group setting where all of the other participants were his stooges, and all gave a clearly incorrect answer. The test subject sat at the end of the row and was asked last which line he thought was the right one. Asch found that, on average, about a third of participants conformed to the clearly incorrect majority, with around three-quarters of participants conforming at least once, although the other quarter never conformed.

When he asked conformers why they had gone along with the wrong answer, some of them admitted it was to fit in with the group, and some said it was because they thought the group was better informed than they were. Here, apparently, was clear experimental evidence of the power of the pressure to conform, and of the susceptibility of ordinary people to that power.

Child of its time?

Asch's experiment has since been extensively criticized for what psychologists call its low 'ecological validity', which basically means the experimental set-up is highly artificial and doesn't represent the real world. It also seems likely that the effect Asch found was 'a child of its time', in that early 1950s America was a time of conformity. The radical social changes of the 1960s and 1970s, with increasing individualism, mean that the conformity effect might no longer apply, and a British replication of Asch's experiment in 1980 found that in only 1 out of 396 trials did someone conform to the incorrect majority.

Despite its limitations, Asch's conformity experiment had raised profound questions about susceptibility to conformity pressure. What were the limits of such pressure? One of the most famous experiments in psychology set out to test one particular strain of conformity: obedience to authority. In the wake of the 1960 trial in Jerusalem of Adolf Eichmann, one of the architects of the Holocaust, American social psychologist Stanley Milgram wanted to test the premise 'that Eichmann and his million accomplices in the Holocaust were just following orders. Could we call them all accomplices?'

The Zimbardo prison experiment

An even more notorious experiment at Stanford University in 1971 further examined the limits and power of conformity. American psychologist Philip Zimbardo converted the basement of the Stanford University psychology department into a makeshift prison and advertised for healthy young men to take part in a prison experiment for $15 a day.

The participants were randomly divided into guards and prisoners. Those assigned to the prisoner group underwent mock arrests and realistic incarceration procedures, while the guards were issued uniforms, truncheons and mirrored glasses. All participants knew that the groups had been randomly assigned, and were informed they could stop participating at any time.

What happened next was extraordinary, as the participants very quickly came to inhabit their roles. The 'prisoners' behaved like real prisoners, and the guards became increasingly autocratic and brutal. The experiment was supposed to run for two weeks but Zimbardo felt forced to shut it down after six days. The dramatic results seemed to demonstrate that individual personality traits are readily subsumed by the demands of a role like 'guard' or 'prisoner', and that institutionalization by itself has profound psychological consequences. Though severely limited in sample size and replicability, and extensively critiqued since, Zimbardo's prison experiment offers powerful evidence for the dehumanizing potential of certain institutions and roles.

Milgram's obedience experiment

Milgram found that, when instructed to do so by an experimenter, most test participants were willing to apply increasingly powerful shocks to a 'learner', even when they could hear shouts and screams of pain from next door. Two-thirds of the participants applied a shock level marked 'danger – severe shock'. Many of them protested but the experimenter followed a script giving prompts (called 'prods') ranging from 'The experiment requires you to continue' to 'You have no other choice but to continue'. 'The extreme willingness of adults to go to almost any lengths on the command of an authority', Milgram reflected, 'constitutes the chief finding of the study and the fact most urgently demanding explanation.'

Why do we fall in love?

'Love is a many-splendored thing', according to a popular song and eponymous movie from 1955. The psychologist's slightly less romantic refrain might be that 'love is a multifactorial thing'. Those factors include initial judgements of physical, emotional and mental attraction, self-concepts of attractiveness, compatibility and how it is assessed, and sociobiology.

Similars attract

Sociobiology is the study of biological, particularly evolutionary, aspects of social behaviour. Sociobiologists argue that although love sounds like an abstract, metaphysical concept, it has its roots in biology and thus in evolution. Studies have revealed some fascinating aspects of the sociobiology of love, particularly around the relationship between compatibility and genetic make-up. Evidence shows that the most powerful force determining compatibility is similarity; people who are more similar are more likely to find each other attractive. This applies from cultural attributes, such as political affiliation or taste in music, down to invisible aspects of biology, such as finger length and even the level of certain gases in the bloodstream.

The smell of love

But in one realm of genetics, the genetics of disease resistance, complementarity trumps compatibility, and it seems that women in particular can determine the most complementary genomes by sense of smell. According to research by Rachel Herz and Elizabeth Cahill at Philadelphia's Monell Chemical Senses Center in 1997, 'for females, how someone smells is the single most important variable [in choosing a lover]'. There is strong evidence that women can pick up incredibly subtle but definite olfactory cues that tell them whether someone has the 'best' genes for them (where 'best' means the genes that most favour disease resistance).

An unusual demonstration of this grew out of research with mice, which have been shown to use scent as a means of determining mate choice. To see whether smell was the signalling mechanism in humans as well, a team at the University of Bern, in Switzerland, led by zoologist Claus Wedekind in 1995, devised a simple test using T-shirts. A group of men were given T-shirts and told to sleep in them for two nights. The T-shirts were then put in boxes with 'smell holes' cut into them, and a group of women were given the boxes to smell and rate according to which smelt 'sexiest'.

The disease-resistance genes of all the participants were sequenced and the results compared with the preferences indicated by the women. Wedekind discovered that women preferred the T-shirts of men whose disease-resistance genes were most different to their own. These also turned out to be the T-shirts they said smelt most like their partners, suggesting that they really were using this method to select partners. Crucially, the women in the experiment were not taking birth control pills and were ovulating (that is, at their most fertile) when the experiment was performed. The Swiss team concluded that pheromones in the men's sweat were mediating signals about their genetic make-up – signals that the women were able to pick up.

Love triangle

One of the most popular theories about love is Robert Sternberg's triangular model. Sternberg identifies three main components of love and claims that different forms of love reflect different combinations of these components. The three components are passion, intimacy and commitment:

Passion: This is the component that is strongest at the start of a romantic relationship. It includes sexual excitement and attraction ('chemistry') and euphoric romantic feelings.

Intimacy: This component develops in the second stage of a relationship as partners open up to one another and share their thoughts, feelings, needs and fears. Intimacy is about feeling close to and secure with your partner.

Commitment: This is the component that develops as a relationship becomes mature. Commitment is about feeling loyal to your partner and to your relationship; about stability, security and belonging.

Assuming that each component can be present or not present, this gives eight possible combinations, each of which Sternberg associates with a particular style of relationship:

Non-love: None of the three components is present.

Infatuation: Passion only.

Liking: Intimacy only.

Empty love: Commitment only.

Romantic love: Passion and intimacy but no commitment.

Companionate love: Intimacy and commitment but no passion.

Fatuous love: Passion and commitment but no intimacy.

Consummate love: All three components are present. Sternberg believed everyone should aspire to 'consummate love', but also argued that couples will be compatible if they share congruency – that is, a similar view of their relationship.

Can you remember being born?

The answer to this question is 'no', even if you believe otherwise. Some people claim memories of birth or the early months of life, but in fact infantile or childhood amnesia is one of the oldest and most robustly observed phenomena in psychology. The earliest memories that can be recalled come after the first two years; memories from before this are probably confabulated (the psychologist's term for 'made up') or appropriated from other people.

Forgotten years

Infantile amnesia was first described in a psychological journal in 1893, and has been reliably demonstrated several times since. Generally there are no memories from birth until the ages of two to three (the average age of earliest memory is around three to three-and-a-half years old), and then few memories – fewer than would be expected through normal forgetting – until around age seven. Either infant memories are not laid down or recall is blocked for some reason; or perhaps something happens to the infant brain that wipes or overwrites the memories.

Remarkable amnesia

Freud believed in the second of these three alternatives, arguing that early memories are encoded but that recall of them is blocked. He described the phenomenon as 'the remarkable amnesia of childhood', and interpreted it as evidence that backed up his theories about sex, repression and the development of the personality. Freud believed that infancy is the scene of tremendous psychic dramas revolving around sex: that young children are exposed to a series of traumatic psychosexual experiences (such as 'castration anxiety'), and that infantile amnesia results from the active suppression of these early experiences, and is therefore the result of sexual and emotional repression. His theory was controversial in the early twentieth century and is widely dismissed by psychologists today.

Cognitive theories suggest that infantile memories are not encoded at all – at least, not in a form that is accessible once we get older. One possibility is that without language, the infant mind does not have the tools to conceptualize memories or make associations; perhaps the lack of a developed sense of self is a similar stumbling block. But such cognitive explanations cannot account for the finding that other species, including rats and mice, have also been shown to exhibit infantile amnesia.

Wipe out

What is more, studies on both rat and human babies show that even very young infants can learn and form memories. So perhaps the third alternative is the correct explanation: something is happening to wipe or overwrite the memories. Studies by Sheena Josselyn and Paul Frankland at the Hospital for Sick Children in Toronto in 2013 suggest that the culprit is the birth of new cells (a process known as 'neurogenesis') in a crucial memory-regulating part of the brain, the hippocampus. This brain region is known to be involved with 'episodic memory' (memory for events), especially autobiographical memory. In rats, mice and humans the hippocampus is the site of extensive neurogenesis, but the rate of generation of new cells drops off sharply with age.

Frankland and Josselyn found evidence that as neurogenesis declines, the availability of long-term memories increases. They showed that artificially boosting neurogenesis in adult rats leads to memory loss while, conversely, species that are born with mature brains and experience little neurogenesis, such as the guinea pig, do not show infantile amnesia. Neurogenesis in the hippocampus is essential to equip children with the ability to learn and store memories when they are slightly older, suggesting that infantile amnesia is the price of a good memory.

Why do babies cry so much?

It may seem obvious that babies cry because they need to signal hunger or some other need, and they cannot speak. However, most parents of young infants can probably quite happily imagine a world where babies use a less distressing – and quieter – mode of communication. So an explanation of infant crying needs to go further.

Monsters of the id

In Freud's account of the development of the personality, the infant psyche is pure, raw id, consisting exclusively of desires and needs. It has no ego boundaries, which is to say, no sense of any boundaries between the self and the rest of the universe, and hence makes no differentiation between personal needs and desires, and the external world that must gratify them. The process of learning that the universe does not correspond to the internal self, so that having a desire is not synonymous with its gratification – in effect discovering that the world does not revolve around you – is inevitably excruciatingly painful in both psychic and physical senses. Perhaps it's no wonder the baby cries, when according to this model its existence is a sort of continuous trauma.

Attachment theory

Freud's account was largely speculative, for all that he claimed it was based on evidence, and offers no insight into the possible function of crying. In developmental psychology, the branch of psychology concerned with how mind and behaviour develop and change throughout life, the predominant model of infant thinking and behaviour has been based on the attachment theory of British psychiatrist John Bowlby.

After the Second World War, Bowlby was commissioned by the World Health Organization to study the effects on children's psychology of being brought up in orphanages, and he theorized that attachment to a maternal figure in the first two years of life is essential for healthy psychological development. Bowlby was influenced by the work in 1937 of Austrian ethologist Konrad Lorenz, which investigated innate mechanisms by which newborn animals attached to their parents. Bowlby believed that humans also have hard-wired, instinctive attachment-enhancing behaviours, and that crying is one of them. In attachment theory, crying is an 'innate releaser' – it releases innate parenting behaviours in adults. Adults have built-in, automatic triggers that are set off by the crying of an infant, and these cue the performance of care-giving behaviours.

There is evidence that adult brains may well be hard-wired to respond to infant cries. A 2012 study by Kate Young and Christine Parsons of Oxford University used brain imaging to monitor brain activity in adults who heard a baby cry. They found that the sound triggered an instant burst of activity, followed by an intense reaction after 100 milliseconds, with extensive activity in parts of the brain linked to the generation of emotion. Other sounds did not produce such an intense reaction. 'This might be a fundamental response present in all of us, regardless of parental status,' commented Parsons.

Driven to action

A second theory of crying is derived from learning theory in behaviourism, and views crying as a 'negative reinforcer'. This is a stimulus that produces a response intended to stop or limit the stimulus; in other words, crying is supposed to be unpleasant for parents to listen to, because this motivates them to act to stop the crying by meeting the baby's needs. The problem with this is that it is simpler to escape an aversive stimulus than act to stop it, so on this basis infant crying could easily be counterproductive. A third theory is that crying is designed to cause 'sympathetic distress', in which a listening adult experiences an involuntary and intense emotional response. This generates feelings of sympathy, which in turn elicits altruism and helpful behaviour.

Evolutionary melodrama

A fourth type of explanation comes from the perspective of sociobiology (the study of how behaviours give evolutionary benefits). According to the 1972 theory of American sociobiologist Robert Trivers, infant crying may be a kind of act (though obviously not consciously intended): a melodramatic way of using physical distress signals, ostensibly linked to breathing difficulties, to deceive parents into oversupplying resources (that is, food and care). Babies who evolved to 'fool' their parents into thinking they were in respiratory distress would get more food, have higher chances of survival, and be more likely to pass on their genes to the next generation.

❉

Why do children copy their parents?

Children copy their parents because they identify with them, using them as models from whom they can learn behaviours, and seeking their approval by modelling themselves in this way.

The bridge

This is the explanation offered by Albert Bandura's 'social learning' theory, an influential approach to learning from the 1960s and 1970s. Often seen as a bridge between behaviourism and cognitive psychology, social learning theory also incorporates elements of Freudian psychology.

In behaviourism, learning is a process of conditioning, in which a response to a stimulus is either positively or negatively reinforced. Positive reinforcement strengthens the association between the stimulus and the particular response, and once that association has been conditioned, learning has taken place. The organism in the middle is essentially a black box. What goes on between its ears, when processing the stimulus to trigger the response, is irrelevant or insignificant, or both.

Modelling

Bandura's social learning approach introduces cognition. Between the stimulus and the response, mental processes occur, allowing 'modelling' to take place. Modelling is the observation of other people's attitudes and behaviours, noting the outcomes of those behaviours, and using this as the basis for your own behaviour. 'Most human behaviour is learned observationally through modelling,' wrote Bandura, 'from observing others, one forms an idea of how new behaviours are performed, and on later occasions this coded information serves as a guide for action.' Modelling requires attention, to direct you to the target behaviour; memory, in encoding and recalling the behaviour; and motivation, to drive the process. These are all cognitive processes.

Bandura also borrowed from Freud in explaining the motivation part of the process. When we model ourselves on one person in particular, Bandura said we identify with them, which involves adopting not just their behaviours but also their beliefs, attitudes and values. In Freudian psychology, 'identification' is a process that boosts self-esteem because the target of the identification is someone we admire and from whom we seek approval. Bandura saw the process in similar terms, although he stressed that we can identify with anyone (whereas Freud was much more restrictive).

Bobo dolls

The best known experimental demonstration of social learning offered by Bandura was the Bobo doll study. A Bobo doll is a person-sized dummy painted as a clown, with a round bottom so that it will roll upright if knocked down.

In the study, those children who saw an adult model playing aggressively with the Bobo doll were more likely to reproduce the behaviour later (by beating a smaller Bobo doll), and in later experiments even seeing a video of an aggressive model stimulated aggressive behaviour. Boys were found to be more aggressive than girls, and both boys and girls were more likely to copy aggressive behaviour from a male model than a female one.

Bandura concluded that the children were learning from the adult model, and the experiment also had obvious implications for the issue of whether exposure to violence in the media triggers violent behaviour. But

his experiment has since been criticized for lacking 'ecological validity', which is to say, it used an unrealistic scenario not reflective of real-life situations. In particular, critics suggest that the children's 'aggressive' behaviour was not true aggression (when beating the Bobo doll the children often behaved like it was a big joke), and that they were simply reflecting the 'demand characteristics' of the experiment, which is to say, they were doing what they thought they were supposed to do in the context of the experiment.

When do children realize that they don't disappear when they cover their eyes?

Up until around ages three to four years, children believe that they cannot be seen by others if they cover their eyes. This 'peekaboo' phenomenon may seem like little more than a charming childhood misconception, but the ability to imagine what others can see – and hence to know that just because you can't see others doesn't mean they can't see you – is one of the core components of the human mind and among the crowning glories of the evolution of human intelligence. When a child is able to think about what others can see, it marks a profound transition to an advanced level of cognition, which marks humans out from the rest of the animal world and opens new worlds of thought and behaviour that were probably crucial to the evolution of our species.

What is it that allows a child to imagine what other people might be able to see (and by extension, think)? Psychologists call it 'theory of mind': a set of mental tools or rules that allow you to put yourself in someone else's shoes. Every time you think about other people, what they might say or do or feel, how they might react, and how you will come across, you are employing theory of mind. Because it involves everyday psychologizing of the sort everyone engages in constantly, it is sometimes called simply 'folk psychology'.

Naughty Anne

The term 'theory of mind' was coined by two primatologists, David Premack and Guy Woodruff, in a 1978 paper in which they wondered, 'Does the chimpanzee have a theory of mind?' Their tests showed that, for instance, if a chimp had to decide who to ask for food – someone who can see where the food is, versus someone blindfolded – they chose no better than if guessing at random. In other words they were not able to theorize about the mental state of the blindfolded person, and thus work out that he could not see the food.

Can children fare any better? A key study tested children for their ability to attribute false beliefs: that is, to understand that someone else might believe something they know to be false. In the 'Sally-Anne' test, a child is shown a little play involving two dolls, Sally and Anne. Anne watches Sally hide a ball in a basket; Sally leaves, Anne moves the ball to a box, and when Sally returns the child is asked, 'Where will Sally look for the ball?' Children under three generally say that Sally will look in the box; children over four correctly impute to Sally the false belief that the ball is still in the basket. They have developed a theory of mind.

Eye see you

Similarly, children over four will be able to understand that just because they cannot see, it doesn't mean that other people cannot see them. But theory of mind may not be the whole story behind the peekaboo phenomenon. Research by James Russell and colleagues at Cambridge University showed that for children the crucial factor is that the eyes cannot be seen, or rather gazed into, by others. In other words, the children held the belief that to be seen by someone, direct eye contact is necessary: 'It would seem that children apply the principle of joint attention to the self and assume that for somebody to be perceived, experience must be shared and mutually known to be shared, as it is when two pairs of eyes meet.'

How do children learn to read?

In contrast to the apparently effortless process of learning to talk (*see* page 80), which seems to come so naturally that the existence of a hard-wired language-acquisition module has been hypothesized, learning to read can be very hard indeed. The traditional view of how we learn to read is that we learn to 'decode' – that is, to learn the relationships between sounds and letters or letter combinations, and to apply these in order to translate written words into sounds. This seems to be true for most children, but it is not necessarily the whole story.

Like riding a bike

With language decoding, children learn a whole set of rules governing the translation of 'graphemes' (letters and combinations of letters) into 'phonemes' (sounds). For instance, they might be taught that an 'A' in the middle of a word with a silent 'E' at the end makes a long sound, as in 'late'. But in English and many other languages, rules fail to encapsulate all aspects of the task, and it may be that children are actually working out probabilistic relationships between graphemes and phonemes, rather than simply memorizing rules. In this sense it could be that learning to read is less like memorizing rules and more like acquiring a skill, similar to riding a bicycle or catching a ball.

Precocious readers

There is also a whole class of readers who did not learn via incremental decoding, but seem to have picked up reading in a fashion more akin to language acquisition. Known as 'precocious readers', these are children who learn to read fluently by age four, and they account for up to 1 per cent of children entering the first year of school. Precocious readers are self-taught, having received no formal or structured tuition, but they are not necessarily highly intelligent. They have little in common as a group beyond coming from literate homes where reading is common and valued.

The existence of precocious readers has been taken as evidence to support the school of thought known as natural learning, which argues that reading should not be taught as a set of incremental rules to train children in decoding ('process-centred learning'). Rather, children should be guided to teach themselves to read, probably by initially learning to recognize whole words and, crucially, privileging meaning over the phonetic rules of decoding ('meaning-centred learning'). The rules of decoding come later, and can be inferred by the child who can already grasp meaning and thus enjoy reading more.

The Reading Wars

The opposing view, championed by the phonics movement, is that for the majority of children, training in decoding achieves superior results. The clash between teaching styles has been dubbed the 'Reading Wars', and the general consensus is that the phonics movement has won, based on the hard evidence of educational achievement when the two strategies are experimentally studied. It may be that in the classroom environment, with high child-to-teacher ratios, natural learning is inappropriate and counterproductive.

Yet even with phonics, millions of children struggle to learn to read, and psychologists point to the scale of the task, in cognitive terms. The brain of a child around five years old has to develop what leading reading activist David Boulton calls 'a language simulation module – something that can take instructions and information from an external code and generate an internal experience of language that we can then reflect on and comprehend'. According to Boulton, this decoding has to work at an astonishingly rapid speed of 25 milliseconds per letter-sound: 'It all must happen incredibly fast.'

Battle for bandwidth

This highly demanding task requires all of the child's cognitive 'bandwidth', but children of this age simultaneously have to deal with another cognitive challenge that also consumes bandwidth: emotional regulation, which profoundly affects attention. According to leading American child psychologist Dr Mark Greenberg, 'Children who have difficulties maintaining attention are often children who also have difficulties regulating their emotions.' This in turn leads to children developing negative attributions (such as 'I'm no good at this') and, says Greenberg, 'those distractions diminish their ability to actually do the task they're struggling with'.

In other words, learning to read is about more than just mastering the rules of decoding; it involves overcoming an interlocking complex of challenges, including emotional regulation, attention and memory. Perhaps unsurprisingly, as many as one out of every five children has a significant reading disability, according to the United States' National Center for Learning Disabilities, with the most common reading disorder, dyslexia, affecting 13 to 14 per cent of the school-aged population, according to the International Dyslexia Association.

Why are teenagers ratty?

Erik Erikson, one of the leading figures of the psychoanalytic movement after Freud, in 1956 called this the 'psychopathology of everyday adolescence' – the stereotypical teenage behaviour of withdrawal, moodiness and defiance.

The Eight Ages of Man

For Erikson, the adolescent phase of the life cycle formed one of the key stages in his influential and popular 'psychosocial theory', an account of the different stages through which each individual passes, and of the psychic challenges they must overcome at each point. His 1959 theory is sometimes known as the 'Eight Ages of Man'. Erikson said that adolescence is characterized by a conflict between identity and role confusion, and that to resolve this conflict the individual must achieve a sense of self-identity. This task, he wrote, means finding a 'feeling of being at home in one's body, a sense of knowing where one is going and an inner assurance of anticipated recognition from those who count'.

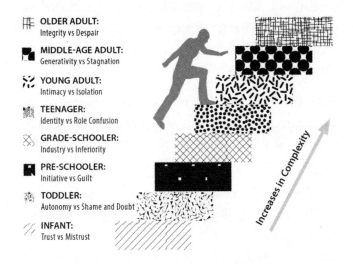

OLDER ADULT:
Integrity vs Despair

MIDDLE-AGE ADULT:
Generativity vs Stagnation

YOUNG ADULT:
Intimacy vs Isolation

TEENAGER:
Identity vs Role Confusion

GRADE-SCHOOLER:
Industry vs Inferiority

PRE-SCHOOLER:
Initiative vs Guilt

TODDLER:
Autonomy vs Shame and Doubt

INFANT:
Trust vs Mistrust

Increases in Complexity

Adolescence is precisely the time when all three of these challenges are at their greatest. To give one example, body image faces one of its greatest crises in adolescence, with rapid growth challenging the sense of mastery of bodily functions that was so hard-won in childhood. At the same time a flood of hormones meets a tide of social and cultural pressures. Changing body image poses particular problems for girls because cultural imperatives are perversely in opposition to biological ones. In girls, puberty causes a greater increase in body fat composition than in boys, who tend to gain muscle mass, but the weight of body image expectation traditionally falls primarily upon girls.

Cultural imperatives stress the need to be thin, even as biology pushes in the opposite direction. According to Erikson, identity confusion in adolescence leads to inevitable identity crisis: 'At no other phase of the lifecycle are the pressures of finding oneself and the threat of losing oneself so closely allied.'

Regression and ambivalence

Leading child psychoanalyst Peter Blos in 1962 described adolescence as a 'second individuation process' (individuation is the process of forging – or perhaps carving – a sense of self-identity separate from others), involving disengagement as the adolescent tries to forge an independent sense of identity. Disengagement produces regression, as when adolescents look for substitute parents through hero worship (for example, of sports or rock stars), and ambivalence. Ambivalence is the tension between dependence and independence, and is a characteristic of early childhood.

In adolescence, ambivalence is reactivated in an extreme form, and it is this which accounts for much of the stereotypical teen's 'ratty' behaviour. The teenager simultaneously needs and rejects parental love and approval. This may take the form of 'negative dependence', in which the adolescent's behaviour remains governed by parental wishes, but in negative (in the photographic sense) – by doing the opposite of what parents want, the teenager nonetheless remains dependent on them. Blos argued that regression is a necessary phase of the adolescent struggle for individuation: an adaptive defence against the temptation to fall back into dependence on adults.

Sturm und Drang?

The main problem with these theories, which belong to what is known in psychology as the 'classical theory of adolescence', is that the evidence shows that, on the whole, teenagers are quite well adjusted. For instance, a 1976 study by the United Kingdom's National Children's Bureau of over 14,000 sixteen-year-olds, found that the vast majority of parents (around 80 to 90 per cent) reported very little conflict with their teenagers over issues such as their choice of friends, evening activities and drinking habits, and that the teenagers' own reports backed this up. So perhaps what G. Stanley Hall, in the founding text of adolescent psychology, *Adolescence* (1904), memorably described as the *Sturm und Drang* ('storm and stress') of teenage years, is more like a storm in a teacup; a popular misconception overhyped by cultural stereotyping.

Why are some folk shy?

'Often before now have I applied my thoughts to the puzzling question,' wrote the Ancient Greek philosopher Theophrastus around 300 BCE, 'why it is that, while all Greece lies under the same sky and all the Greeks are educated alike, it has befallen us to have characters so variously constituted.' Ever since then, people have been wondering about the different types of personality, and where they come from.

Psychological types

Personality types and traits are the domain of the discipline known as differential psychology. As discussed on page 96 ('Why do nice guys finish last?'), differential psychology has identified five major personality dimensions. The best known and, according to some, the most important of these dimensions is introversion–extroversion. Shy folk are said to be introverts; they lie at the introversion end of the dimension.

Typical types

Eysenck characterized the 'typical introvert' as 'a quiet, retiring sort of person, introspective, fond of books rather than people ... reserved and distant except to intimate friends.' Associated characteristics include 'distrust of impulse and excitement ... seriousness ... close control [of emotions] ... [and] reliability.

In contrast, Eysenck said, the typical extrovert is:

> sociable, likes parties, has many friends, needs to have people to talk to ... He craves excitement, takes chances ... acts on the spur of the moment and is generally impulsive ... likes change; he is carefree, easy-going, optimistic ... prefers to keep moving and doing things, tends to be aggressive ... altogether his feelings are not kept under tight control and he is not always a reliable person.

The terms extroversion and introversion were coined by psychoanalyst Carl Jung in his 1921 book *Psychologische Typen* (*Psychological Types*), but the underlying ideas date back to the humours and their associated temperaments of the Classical world (*see* page 9). Choleric and sanguine temperaments were characterized by Wilhelm Wundt (1832–1920), the first psychologist, as 'changeable', and this was later deemed to be equivalent to extroversion by the differential psychologist Hans Eysenck (1916–97), one of the most influential figures in the field.

Arousal and reward

It was Eysenck who, in the late 1940s, adapted Jung's terms to describe a dimension – extroversion–introversion, aka 'E' – which he had identified through statistical analysis of personality data provided by 700 soldiers he was treating (*see* page 147 for a description of the traits of introverts and extroverts). Eysenck believed that such fundamental personality dimensions must have a basis in biology. He argued that the E dimension is based on differences in 'cortical excitability' or 'arousal', the intensity and magnitude of brain activity. Eysenck suggested that introverts have naturally higher levels of cortical arousal, processing information faster, whereas extroverts have lower arousal. Introverts are therefore more sensitive to external stimulus, which can more easily overload their information processing channels, and so behave in such a way as to minimize exposure to stimulus, whereas extroverts seek greater stimulation to compensate for their lower levels of arousal.

A rival theory, called the 'Reinforcement Sensitivity Theory' was proposed by Jeffrey Gray in 1970. He suggested that the basis for the E dimension lies in the way the brain's reward system works, with the brains of extroverts being more sensitive to rewards, such as those triggered by social interactions, so that they are motivated to pursue these rewards. There is experimental evidence for both theories, such as the 'lemon juice' experiment, which shows that introverts salivate more in response to lemon juice because they have higher levels of activity in the part of the brain that regulates cortical arousal, and which responds to taste stimuli.

What do IQ tests really measure?

There is a lot of scepticism surrounding IQ tests, and one of the most common accusations is that IQ tests only test your ability to do well on IQ tests. This accounts for the famous saying of early twentieth-century psychologist Edwin Boring that intelligence should be defined as 'that quality which is measured by intelligence tests'. So should IQ tests be taken seriously? Are they really a good measure of intelligence?

What is an IQ test?

IQ stands for 'intelligence quotient'. Quotient is another word for ratio, so a quotient is the number you get by dividing or comparing one quantity with another. Defining what is meant by intelligence is not so straightforward. In 1994 the American Psychological Association's Task Force on intelligence admitted, 'When two dozen prominent theorists were recently asked to define intelligence, they gave two dozen somewhat different definitions.' The APA itself suggested this definition: '[The] ability to understand complex ideas, to adapt effectively to the environment, to learn from experience, to engage in various forms of reasoning, to overcome obstacles by taking thought.'

Modern IQ tests work by testing several different types of mental ability, such as your ability with words, your ability with numbers, your ability to manipulate shapes in your mind's eye, and your ability to think logically; your scores on these tests are then combined to give an overall score. This score is then compared to the average score, and the result of this calculation gives your IQ. Your IQ is therefore a way of describing your intelligence compared to other people (other adults, to be precise). By definition, an IQ score of 100 is the average – if you achieved a score of 100 on an IQ test it would mean that you were of average intelligence for your age.

What it is not

What IQ is not can be as important as what it is in gaining a better handle on this much-misunderstood concept. IQ is not the same thing as intelligence, although the difference between the two things depends on whom you ask. Some psychologists argue that IQ tests only analyse very specific aspects of intelligence, and that an IQ score is a poor description of someone's overall intelligence because it misses out important aspects such as, for instance, how good they are with people or how good they are with their hands. Others argue that IQ tests are an almost perfect measure of intelligence, and that therefore someone's IQ score is an excellent description of their intelligence.

IQ is *not* a measure of knowledge, wisdom or memory, although these may well be related to your IQ score, just as they may be related to your intelligence. Memory in particular – or at least some types of memory, such as working memory – may play an important role in determining your performance on IQ tests. IQ is *not* a measure of potential, but of performance. Your IQ score is a measure of how you performed on that test at that point. You may have the potential to perform much better.

The g factor

If an IQ test is made up of different types of question, which test different types of mental ability, how can an IQ test be used as a single measure? Aren't the different types of question measuring different things? How can they be combined to give one overall score – isn't that like comparing apples and oranges?

The answer is no – at least, probably not. It turns out that the different types of questions are probably measuring different aspects of the same thing, or at the very least that your ability in these different areas is due in large part to a single common factor. Psychologists call this common factor 'general intelligence', or use the shorthand notation 'g'. Statistical analysis suggests that IQ and g are 90 per cent the same thing (or, to put it in a more technically accurate fashion, that g and IQ are roughly 90 per cent correlated), so that many psychologists use the terms interchangeably.

Does IQ matter?

A common trope of popular wisdom is that IQ testing has little to do with the real world, and that test 'smarts' and being an egghead won't help you to graduate from the 'university of life'. A quick look at typical test questions illustrates why it is easy to dismiss the relevance of IQ tests: talents such as being able to predict that the next shape in a series should be a triangle inside a hexagon, or being able to decode anagrams of collective nouns, don't seem to bear much relation to real-world tasks such as fixing a sink or appraising employees.

The power to predict

The evidence, however, very clearly shows that performance on IQ tests *does* have a lot of relevance to real-world issues, and in particular that it is a good predictor of everything from educational attainment and career success to wealth and health. For instance, it has been shown that people with high IQ scores are more likely to do better at school, secure better and more highly paid jobs and be more successful at them, and also to live longer and stay healthier longer than people with low IQ scores.

Compared to people with an IQ over 110, those with IQ in the 75 to 90 range are 88 times more likely to drop out of school, 5 times more likely to live in poverty and 7 times more likely to end up in jail. At a national level, the average IQ of a country directly correlates to its per capita GDP. A 2011 study published in the journal *Psychological Science* looked at ninety countries and found that the 'intelligence of the [citizens], particularly the smartest 5 per cent, made a big contribution to the strength of their economies'. Per capita GDP went up $229 per point of average IQ, while the effect was even more pronounced when looking at the IQ of the smartest 5 per cent of the population, where every additional IQ point was worth $468 extra to the per capita GDP.

Studies on the use of IQ-style testing as a tool for selecting job applicants show that it is as good at choosing successful employees as detailed, structured interviews, and better than other measures such as years of job experience. It is important to emphasize that no measure has 100 per cent predictive power for such life factors. IQ scores generally have a roughly 30 to 50 per cent predictive power (for the factors mentioned), which means that they can predict up to 50 per cent of the variation in, say, income. This may not sound impressive, but it is better than almost any other available measure. It also brings home, however, that IQ is at best half the story even when we look at the population as a whole.

Person to person

When it comes to individuals, the case is even less clear, because for any one individual other factors can prove much more important. These factors range from your upbringing and childhood environment to your personal motivation and conscientiousness. For instance, someone who scores poorly on IQ tests but is hard-working and perseveres can easily outperform a super-intelligent layabout. It's just that in the population as a whole, this does not generally happen. To sum up, the short answer is yes, IQ tests do measure something useful in the real world – your intelligence and with it a large chunk of your potential to succeed in life.

Are men really from Mars and women from Venus?

John Gray's book *Men Are From Mars, Women Are From Venus* (1992) has sold over 11 million copies in the US alone, and has been translated into forty different languages. Thanks in large part to the astonishing success of Gray's book and others like it, it has become a cliché to claim that there are profound gender differences in psychology. But what are the real differences between male and female minds, and how much do they owe to differences between male and female brains?

Shades of grey

Men's brains are, on average, bigger than women's brains, but simple brain size is not believed to relate to personality. Within the brain, however, over a hundred gender differences have been found. Perhaps the biggest is that men have much more grey matter in their brains and women have much more white matter. Grey matter is composed of the bodies of nerve cells, so it looks like men have more nerve cells, but white matter is composed of the long, fatty fibres that link nerve cells together, so it looks like women have more connections between nerve cells.

What does this mean in practical terms? One suggestion is that grey matter is better for localized processing, and so men are better at focusing on single, specific tasks, while white matter helps with mental networking, making women better at transitioning between mental tasks, and hence at multitasking. In terms of overall intelligence, more white matter might seem to indicate greater processing power, but in fact there are no significant gender differences in overall IQ scores.

His brain, her brain

A 2001 study by researchers at Harvard found that, in women, parts of the brain that are larger included the limbic cortex, which is responsible for regulating emotions, while in men the parietal cortex, which is involved with space perception, is larger on average. Such findings seem to correlate with psychological differences: women are generally deemed to be 'more emotional', and certainly score higher on average on tests of verbal fluency involving discussion of emotion. Men score higher on average on tests of spatial intelligence, such as map reading or mentally rotating shapes.

There are many more specific gender differences in brain structures. Some of them may explain why some mental illnesses are gender-biased. For instance, males are much more likely to suffer from autism and schizophrenia, while depression and chronic anxiety are much more common in females.

Unpicking the difference

However, it would be wrong to confidently claim that metaphorically men and women really are from different planets. For one thing, not everyone agrees that gender differences between brains are so clear-cut. While specific brain structures studied independently may differ, this is not the same as saying that all male brains show one set of gender structures and all females the other. Individual brains are more likely to show a mixture of 'male' and 'female' characteristics, so it might be more accurate to describe brains as 'intersex'.

Secondly, there aren't clear links between differing brain structures and differing behaviours, or vice versa.

Although we can hypothesize that a higher ratio of grey to white matter in male brains makes men better at task-focused projects and gives them tunnel vision, it is very difficult to prove this. Thirdly, disentangling the effects of cultural and social stereotyping from innate differences present at birth (that is, sorting nurture from nature) is almost impossible. For instance, are there far more male engineers because the high grey: white matter ratio makes men better at single-minded focus on engineering problems, or because girls are discouraged from infancy from interest in 'hard sciences' such as maths, physics and engineering?

Finally, the most important thing to appreciate about gender differences is that, on the whole, they are much smaller than the differences between individuals (exceptions to this rule are obvious biological differences and the stereotypes imposed by society). For example, although men may score higher on map-reading tests, on average, the differences between the scores of any particular man and any particular woman are likely to be similar to the differences between two randomly selected men.

Nature or nurture?

In Shakespeare's play *The Tempest*, one of the shipwrecked sailors lambasts the savage Caliban, who seems resistant to all attempts to 'civilize' him: 'On thy foul nature, nurture will never stick.' The debate over the extent to which nature is subject or superior to nurture still rages today, forming one of the central topics of psychology.

Nativists vs empiricists

In psychology the poles of the nature–nurture debate are represented on the one hand by nativists, who believe that all psychology is determined by our genetic programming, and on the other by the empiricists, who believe that the mind begins as a blank slate, and that all cognition and behaviour derives from experience. The behaviourists (*see* page 77) were empiricists, arguing that all behaviour is learned, or rather conditioned, through the action of the environment on the organism. Freud was closer to nativism, arguing that the drives that govern the human psyche and its development are innate. Similarly Bowlby's attachment drive (*see* page 127) and Chomsky's language acquisition device (*see* page 80) were conceptualized as innate – built into our brains by biology, evolution and our genes.

In modern psychology the two camps are sometimes characterized as evolutionary psychology on the nature side and cultural psychology on the nurture side. Paul Rozin of the University of Pennsylvania is a psychologist with a foot in both camps, and in 2004 he explained: 'Basically, there is a turf battle between the two. Moderates on both sides recognize that the other side has a legitimate explanatory role, but the question comes down to how much of an explanatory role. Each side wants the bigger piece of the pie.'

A natural experiment

The field in which the nature–nurture debate has raged most fiercely is intelligence, where the point of contention is the degree to which intelligence (specifically IQ scores) is determined by genetics or the environment. In fact, to ask how much of an individual's intelligence is determined by nature or nurture is to make a 'category error', which is to say, ask a non-sensical question. In 2004, Canadian neuropsychologist Donald Hebb suggested it was equivalent to asking: 'Which contributes more to the area of a rectangle, its length or its width?' But what can be interrogated is the difference between individuals and groups, and what determines the variation between them. The proportion of variance between individuals attributable to genetic differences is termed the heritability estimate.

To estimate heritability with an experiment would require test groups of children to be raised under strictly controlled conditions, an experiment that we can only hope will never be carried out (although see 'Where does language come from?', page 80, for similar experiments on the origins of language). But a striking natural experiment has been extremely influential in the nature–nurture debate: studies of identical twins separated at birth (*see* page 164). Although today twins are not separated for adoption, in the past this has happened, resulting in genetically identical individuals experiencing different environments during their upbringing. If IQ and other attributes are determined by the environment, they should demonstrate wide differences, but if genes are the determinants they should be remarkably similar.

The twin studies led to the widespread assumption that the heritability estimate, at least in regards to IQ, is 80 per cent. But this estimate is now widely regarded as flawed. One reason is that the twin studies themselves may have been flawed – many of the separated twins actually had very similar upbringings and environments. In cases where the twins' upbringings had been very different, so were their IQ scores.

The Minnesota Twins

Among the best-known twin studies is the Minnesota Twin Study started by Thomas Bouchard in the 1970s. Among the extraordinary cases he collected were the 'Jim twins', James Lewis and James Springer, separated weeks after birth, reports of whose lives purported to reveal a host of coincidences. Both had married and divorced women named Linda and then remarried women named Betty. Both worked in law enforcement. They drank, smoked and chewed their fingernails in the same way. Their first-born sons were named James Alan Lewis and James Allan Springer. Even the names of their childhood pets were the same.

Reaction range

One interpretation of the evidence on nature vs nurture is the concept of the 'reaction range'. This is where your genes set the parameters within which you can respond and adapt to the environment (the reaction range), but the environment determines where you will end up within these parameters. For example, your genes for height might set a reaction range between 1.75 and 1.85

metres (5 ft 9 in and 6 ft 1 in), and if you experience optimum nutrition and health in your environment while growing up you will end up at the top of the range. In 1971, Sandra Scarr-Salapatek estimated that for most people, the reaction range for IQ is 20 to 25 points, meaning that any individual's IQ score would be expected to vary by as much as 25 points depending on the environment to which they have been exposed.

Many psychologists now argue that the way to resolve the nature–nurture debate is to focus on the interplay of biology and experience. It is increasingly clear that genetics, neurological structure, experience and disease operate as part of a complex feedback loop. One striking example of this is that you are three times more likely to die from a heart attack if you are depressed than if you are not.

Is grief a mental illness?

In 2013 the American Psychiatric Association published the fifth edition of its *Diagnostic Statistical Manual of Mental Disorders*, known as *DSM-5*. Among many controversial aspects was the removal of a clause which had specified that people grieving for the death of a loved one should not be diagnosed with depression. This sparked a flurry of headlines saying that psychiatrists were now calling grief a mental illness, and that anyone who mourned a lost child, spouse or parent for more than a fortnight would be deemed mentally ill.

The bible of psychiatry

To understand the controversy it is first necessary to understand the status of the *DSM*. Commonly known as 'the bible of psychiatry', the *DSM* is a handbook for defining and classifying mental illnesses, intended to help psychiatrists, psychologists and other health professionals maintain consistency in their diagnosis and treatment. The *DSM* covers illnesses including schizophrenia, depression, personality disorders, bipolar disorder and anxiety. It has come to possess great power because it is so widely used in America and elsewhere, because many health insurers only consider a claim if a diagnosis has a *DSM* code assigned, and because the *DSM* prescribes treatment. If a new edition of the *DSM* opens new areas for drug treatment, for instance by introducing a new disorder for which antidepressants are the indicated therapy, drug companies can make enormous profits from the newly created market.

Although the *DSM* is produced via a careful and exhaustive process undertaken and reviewed by many of America's leading mental health professionals, most of its incarnations have aroused immense controversy. The earliest editions, for instance, classified homosexuality as a pathology, while the enormous increase in the prescription of drugs for mental illness, and the extension of drug therapy to young children, described as the wholesale medicalization of non-pathological areas of psychology, has been widely blamed on *DSM-III* and *IV*. This is the context for the furore over the removal of the 'bereavement exclusion' clause in diagnosis of depression, which has led to widespread accusations that *DSM-5* is attempting to pathologize grief.

Reasons not to be cheerful

In fact, many of these accusations are false and misleading. There is, for instance, no time limit set, after which bereavement grief is considered pathological. The committee behind *DSM-5* was asked to consider why a diagnosis of depression should have a bereavement exclusion when there are no such exclusions for other traumatic life events, such as divorce or loss of a job. Just because someone is grieving does not mean they cannot be in the grip of clinical depression. What *DSM-5* now allows is that bereavement grief can be considered a mental illness when it is prolonged and severe, pervasive and debilitating, and in particular when suicidal thoughts or behaviours are present. While most bereaved people show grief reactions within a typical range, 10 to 15 per cent have very severe reactions that may justify treatment by medication and counselling.

Supporters of the change frame the dropping of the bereavement exclusion as no longer denying depressed patients badly needed treatment avenues simply because they are bereaved. Opponents point out that up to 80 per cent of antidepressants are prescribed by primary care physicians (for example family doctors) rather than psychiatrists, and that these physicians are often hard-pressed, time-limited and poorly trained in the fine psychological judgement needed to discern grief from depression. 'Anticipate the worst. If something can be misused, it will be misused,' warned Dr Allen Frances, who headed the task force behind *DSM-IV*, published in 1994. Speaking to National Public Radio in the United States, Frances predicted, 'If diagnosis can lead to over-diagnosis and over-treatment, that will happen. So you need to be very, very cautious in making changes that may open the door for a flood of fad diagnoses.'

How can you spot a psychopath?

'Psychopathy' is a personality disorder characterized by low levels of emotional empathy, high levels of impulsivity, narcissism and sensation-seeking, and a reckless disregard for consequences. A 'psychopath' (the term preferred by clinical psychologists, although the related term 'sociopath' is also sometimes used) is someone who exhibits a constellation of typical behaviours, characteristics and attitudes. Presumably such a dysfunctional and dangerous person should be easy to spot; surely you wouldn't have to spend long in the company of a serial killer, for instance, to have a pretty good idea of his or her nature?

In fact, spotting a psychopath is not that easy. Firstly, psychopathy is a spectrum, not a disease that you either have or don't have. All of us are located somewhere on the spectrum; a clinically diagnosed psychopath is someone at the extreme end. Secondly, psychopaths are much more common than you probably realize. About 1 per cent of the population have high levels of psychopathy, and although psychopaths are vastly more likely to end up as criminals, psychopathic traits can also contribute to success in many fields. It is suspected, for instance, that many top business leaders are successful precisely because of, rather than in spite of, high levels of psychopathy. So you might encounter a psychopath in everyday life, or even be working for one!

The mask of sanity

In his landmark 1941 book *The Mask of Sanity*, American psychiatrist Hervey M. Cleckley identified sixteen factors that are still viewed as the essential components of psychopathy, including: superficial charm and good intelligence; unreliability; untruthfulness and insincerity; lack of remorse or shame; antisocial behaviour; poor judgement and failure to learn from experience; pathological egocentricity and incapacity for love; impersonal sexual relations; and failure to follow any life plan.

Building on this, criminal psychologist Robert Hare created what is now widely known as 'the psychopath test', technically known as the 'PCL-R' – a tool for clinicians to assess the degree of psychopathy. Subjects are rated from 0 (doesn't apply) to 2 (fully applies) on twenty criteria, including glibness and superficial charm, grandiose sense of self-worth, pathological lying, being cunning or manipulative, lack of remorse, emotional shallowness, callousness and lack of empathy, unwillingness to accept responsibility for actions, a tendency to boredom, a parasitic lifestyle, a lack of realistic long-term goals, impulsivity, irresponsibility, lack of behavioural control, behavioural problems in early life, juvenile delinquency, criminal versatility, multiple marriages and promiscuous sexual behaviour. The maximum possible score is 40, which indicates a pure, prototypical psychopath, but anyone scoring over 30 would qualify for clinical diagnosis of psychopathy. Hare counsels against non-professionals using the checklist to attempt amateur diagnoses.

The psychopath quiz

You can get a tentative idea of where you fall on the psychopathy spectrum with the following short quiz. Score 0 for disagree strongly, 1 for agree somewhat and 2 for agree strongly:

Rules are for suckers

I look after number one – after all, it's a dog eat dog world

Lying is OK if it gets you what you want

Responsibilities are a pointless burden

I never regret anything

I live for the moment: the past is gone and the future can take care of itself

I can be extremely charming when I want to

I often act on the spur of the moment

I've had my share of trouble with authority

I get bored easily

Someone scoring over 15 might be rated as having psychopathic tendencies, although this could only be confirmed by a clinical psychologist, or equivalent mental health professional.

What is normal?

The medical aspect of psychology – the area in which psychiatrists (doctors who specialize in mental health) work – is sometimes called abnormal psychology. In slightly circular fashion, abnormal psychology is defined as the study of abnormal behaviour and cognition. But defining abnormality means defining, or setting limits to, normality.

'The four Ds'

The question of what constitutes abnormal and what is normal is profoundly important in both theory and practice. It is the basis of *The Diagnostic and Statistical Manual of Mental Disorders* (*DSM*) and all other diagnostic systems, and governs the health status and treatment of millions of people. There is no universally accepted definition of abnormal, but most practitioners agree on an approach governed by 'the four Ds': deviance, distress, dysfunction and danger.

'Deviance' refers to thoughts and behaviour deemed to deviate from social norms, although this criterion is inevitably fraught with cultural and historical subjectivity. Homosexuality and feminism have been and are still considered deviant in many societies and cultures. Specific circumstances can also change what should be considered normal by society; for instance, an outburst of violence could be considered normal in extreme circumstances such as a wartime situation. Extreme reactions to extreme circumstances are arguably more 'normal' than measured reactions.

Manics and ultramarathons

'Distress' refers to the notion that unusual thoughts and behaviours must cause distress before they can be considered abnormal. Some people subject themselves to extreme fasting, purgative regimes, physical self-abuse and exhaustive dancing in order to engage in mystical-religious rituals; these are unusual behaviours, but they can provide enormous spiritual satisfaction. If you read of a man who forced himself to run across a baking desert on blistered feet day after day, you might think he was mentally ill, but what if you learned he was taking part in an ultramarathon, such as the Marathon des Sables, in which participants run the equivalent of five and a half marathons in five or six days? Another confounding scenario is when lack of distress, in the form of a disproportionate sense of well-being, is actually a symptom of a mental disorder, as in mania, characterized by extreme euphoria.

Eccentricity checklist

David Weeks, who carried out a landmark study on eccentrics in 1995, estimated that around two in 10,000 people qualify as 'classic, full-time eccentrics'. Here's his checklist: having ten or more of these characteristics would categorize you as eccentric.

Nonconforming

Creative

Strongly curious

Idealistic

Happily obsessed with a hobby (or more than one)

Aware of being different from others since early childhood

Intelligent

Opinionated and outspoken

Uncompetitive

Unusual eating or lifestyle habits

Lack of interest in others or being with them

Mischievous sense of humour

Single

Eldest or only child

Poor at spelling

'Dysfunction' refers to the impact of thoughts and behaviours on everyday life. Imagine someone who has intense hallucinations but has no problem maintaining a healthy, functioning family life and job: are they mentally ill? 'Danger' is seen as the ultimate marker of abnormality, referring to behaviour that causes a person to be a danger to him- or herself or others. But this is extremely rare, and so will not apply to the vast majority of cases.

As you can see, most of 'the four D' criteria raise problems and ambiguities, yet they could form the basis for deciding on interventions, which may be extreme and invasive. One of the most problematic categories of person is the eccentric individual: someone whose behaviour is deviant and possibly dysfunctional, but who does not need treatment. Eccentrics are differentiated from those with mental disorders by issues such as freedom of choice and contentment (*see* opposite).

Why do soldiers get flashbacks?

Flashbacks are a symptom of the conditions known as 'acute stress disorder' and 'post-traumatic stress disorder' (PTSD), which are caused by exposure to trauma such as combat, rape, disasters, abuse, assault or accidents.

Shell shock and combat fatigue

Combat-related anxiety disorders that manifest during combat have been recognized in one form or another for hundreds of years. During the American Civil War this was known as 'nostalgia', because it was believed that homesickness was the root of the problem. In the First World War, 'shell shock' was believed to have an organic cause in tiny brain haemorrhages or concussions caused by explosions, and in the Second World War and the Korean War affected soldiers were said to be suffering from 'combat fatigue'. Recognition of anxiety and depression disorders occurring and persisting after combat only emerged in the wake of the Vietnam War, when it became apparent that up to 29 per cent of combat veterans – and up to 80 per cent of prisoner of war veterans – suffered severe symptoms after returning home. These symptoms were eventually classified as either acute stress disorder or PTSD.

Acute stress disorder is severe anxiety and/or depression that begins within four weeks of a traumatic event and lasts for less than a month, while if symptoms persist for more than a month, the diagnosis changes to PTSD. PTSD can start soon after an event or many years later, and can persist indefinitely. A 2009 study in the *Journal of the American Geriatrics Society*, which interviewed 157 Second World War veterans who had been prisoners of war, found that they still suffered traumatic memories and clinical levels of PTSD sixty-five years after their captivity.

Symptoms of PTSD

Acute stress disorder and PTSD differ only in terms of onset and duration. Their symptoms are identical, and include 'flashbacks', 'avoidant behaviour', 'reduced responsiveness' (leading to so-called 'psychic numbness' and 'dissociation', or 'psychological separation'), increased sensitivity, problems with concentration and feelings of guilt.

Flashbacks, or re-experiencing the traumatic event, can occur through dreams, waking memories or even vivid hallucinations that cause the person to relive the event as if it were going on. These flashbacks can be triggered by a huge range of stimuli. Studies of Vietnam veterans with PTSD showed that simple events such as hot days or sudden downpours, reminiscent of conditions in Vietnam, could cause flashbacks, as could combat scenes in any media. PTSD sufferers often work to avoid possible triggers and modify their thinking and behaviour accordingly.

What could be going on in the brains of those suffering flashbacks? A 2008 brain imaging study showed that the brains of people with stress-related disorders not only have to work harder to accomplish memory tasks, but are less active during a suppression task than the brains of healthy people. When asked, in effect, not to think about something, the stress-related disorder sufferers showed less activity in the prefrontal cortex, suggesting problems with the parts of the brain involved in preventing traumatic memories from surfacing.

Flashbacks can be extremely frightening, and trigger dangerous behaviour. One tale related in the magazine *Psychology Today* tells of a Vietnam veteran who was driving on the freeway when a helicopter passed low overhead. Before he knew it, he had pulled over, jumped out of the car and thrown himself into a ditch, as a flashback triggered an automatic 'cover' reaction. Advice on how to deal with a flashback includes trying to regulate your breathing, attempting to ground yourself in the present through using all five senses and even literally stamping your feet on the ground.

Is it better not
to feel so much?

The biggest story in mental health since the 1970s has been the explosive growth in drug therapy. Adverse effects, poor monitoring and doubtful efficacy are major bones of contention with psychiatric drug therapy, but there are also more profound, philosophical objections to the use of drugs to treat issues such as grief, melancholy, anxiety, mania and hyperactivity. These can be seen as extreme but natural aspects of the human condition, raising questions about whether it is right to medicate them.

Zombies and Stepford Wives

Antidepressant use in the United States rose by nearly 400 per cent between 1990 and 2011, according to the Centers for Disease Control and Prevention's National Center for Health Statistics, with 11 per cent of Americans over the age of twelve taking an antidepressant, and about 14 per cent taking one for more than ten years. One of many side effects reported from the use of antidepressants, particularly the class known as SSRIs (which affect the way neurons deal with the chemical messenger serotonin), is a kind of emotional flattening or dullness, technically known as 'flat affect'. This happens in 10 to 20 per cent of patients on SSRIs (which include Prozac).

Sufferers describe feeling numb, disengaged, levelled out and even, in extreme cases, zombified. Although relatively rare, such experiences have fed into the popular conception of Prozac as somehow antipathetical to the diversity of human experience and emotion, transforming those who take it into 'Stepford Wives'. Prozac is also widely accused of deadening creativity, with the implication being that extremes of mood are necessary for true creativity.

Given such experiences, many people within and outside the mental health profession are seriously sceptical about the virtue of drug therapy. Do drugs relieve symptoms or suppress feelings? Should we really be trying to smother feelings, even distressing ones? The underlying rationale of drug therapy is partly predicated on the contention that mental disorders such as depression are due to chemical imbalances in the brain. In fact there is no definitive evidence that this is true, and little understanding of what it might mean in practice. There is, for instance, no test you can do to check your neurochemical 'balance'. Depression and other disorders have psychological, social and spiritual dimensions; how can drug therapy address these?

Philosophers have had plenty to say on the issue. For instance, in *The Imitation of Christ* (*c.* 1418–27), the German monk Thomas à Kempis opined: 'It is good to encounter troubles and adversities, from time to time; for trouble often compels a man to search his own heart.' The early medieval Roman philosopher Boethius was one of many who argued that adversity is character-forming: 'Good fortune deceives; adverse fortune teaches.'

Pharmacological Calvinism

But there is another side to the argument. The movement castigating people for daring to medicate distressing symptoms was first labelled 'Pharmacological Calvinism' by Dr Gerald Klerman in 1972. Medication is viewed as the easy way out, and a sign of moral and/or temperamental weakness. This rather ascetic viewpoint deems pill-popping to be a way of shirking the hard work of spiritual self-improvement. To some extent it implies a dualist approach to psychology, which is where the mind is seen as separate from the body, denying the materiality of the mind. If mind is immaterial then mental problems cannot have organic causes – and by extension, they cannot be treated with drugs or any other material therapy.

Many psychotherapists stress the pragmatic approach to drug therapy. Dr Ron Pies, clinical professor of psychiatry at Tufts University School of Medicine, Boston, in 2009 pointed out that 'depression itself often leads to a blunting of emotional reactivity and an inability to feel the ordinary pleasures and sorrows of life . . . [putting] the question of antidepressant side effects in perspective: how bad could the side effects be, in comparison with severe depression itself?' Pies offers the homily that 'Medication is just a bridge between feeling awful and feeling better. You still need to move your legs and walk across that bridge!' As for the notion that drug therapy undermines the basis of creativity, this is strongly refuted by the many artists who claim the exact opposite. There is even a whole book, *Poets on Prozac* (2008), dedicated to dispelling this myth.

Further reading

Bayne, Tim (ed); *Oxford Companion to Consciousness* (OUP, 2009)

Comer, Ronald J.; *Abnormal Psychology* (8th edition) (Worth Publishers, 2012)

Craighead, W. Edward (ed); *Concise Corsini Encyclopaedia of Psychology and Behavioral Science* (Wiley, 2004)

Davey, Graham; *Encyclopaedic Dictionary of Psychology* (Hodder Education, 2006)

Gregory, Richard (ed); *The Oxford Companion to the Mind* (2nd edition) (OUP, 2004)

Harre, Rom; *Key Thinkers in Psychology* (Sage, 2005)

Hopkins, Brian (ed); *Cambridge Encyclopaedia of Child Development* (Cambridge, 2005)

Kurtz, Lester (ed); *Encyclopaedia of Violence, Peace and Conflict* (Elsevier, 2008)

Levy, Joel; *Why? Answers to Everyday Scientific Questions* (Michael O'Mara Books, 2012)

McLeish, Kenneth (ed); *Bloomsbury Guide to Human Thought* (Bloomsbury, 1993)

Nadel, L; *Encyclopaedia of Cognitive Science* (Wiley, 2002)

Rosario, V. A. and Pillard, Richard; *Homosexuality and Science: A Guide to the Debates* (ABC-CLIO, 2002)

Sheehy, N. *et al.* (eds.), *Biographical Dictionary of Psychology* (Routledge, 1997)

Scientific American: The Hidden Mind (2002)

Skelton, Ross (ed); *Edinburgh International Encyclopaedia of Psychoanalysis* (Edinburgh University Press, 2010)

American Psychological Association: www.apa.org

Bethlem Museum of the Mind:
museumofthemind.org.uk

International Society for the Study of Trauma and Dissociation: www.isst-d.org

Learning Theories: www.learning-theories.com

Psych Central: psychcentral.com

Psychology Today magazine:
www.psychologytoday.com

Simply Psychology: www.simplypsychology.org

The History of Phrenology on the Web: John van Wyhe;
www.historyofphrenology.org.uk

The Psychologist: Journal of the British Psychological Society; www.thepsychologist.org.uk

Index